Monkseaton Village
Volume Two

by Charlie Steel

PREFACE

The preface in Monkseaton Village Volume One began with an apology. That apology was made on the basis that any information contained within is only as accurate as the source from which it was obtained.

It is often difficult to guarantee the reliability of historic information unless it has been accurately documented, and sometimes it isn't, so that apology extends to this book – Monkseaton Village Volume Two.

Local History research is fascinating but it is also very time consuming and sometimes confusing.

Searching out information to compile a book might seem straightforward enough, but putting the facts together can be a lot more difficult.

When a conflict of information is encountered it sometimes requires logical interpretation and calculated judgement to process and simplify that information to make it easily understood.

As with Monkseaton Volume One, I have again researched the information for this publication to the best of my ability, and attempted to ensure its accuracy as far as possible, however I am well aware that there will always be some details which may continue to be open to debate, especially those which may not be documented, or are taken from the personal recollections of the contributors.

If any obvious inaccuracies are found, it would be advantageous to advise me along with a provable reference source rather than being critical of the content, and this way with your help, they can be corrected for the benefit of any future editions.

Charlie Steel
November 2012

Previous page: 'The Unwelcome Visitor' – On 3rd August 1934, following a collision with a motor car, this lorry laden with bricks mounted the kerb and crashed through the garden wall of No. 3 Front Street, Monkseaton, (corner of Kenilworth Road). No-one was injured in the accident.

Summerhill Books

Summerhill Books publishes local history books on Northumberland, Durham and Tyneside. To receive a catalogue of our titles send a stamped addressed envelope to:

Andrew Clark, Summerhill Books, PO Box 1210, Newcastle-upon-Tyne NE99 4AH

or email: summerhillbooks@yahoo.co.uk

or visit our website to view our full range of books: **www.summerhillbooks.co.uk**

Copyright Charlie Steel 2012

First published in 2012 by

Summerhill Books
PO Box 1210, Newcastle-upon-Tyne NE99 4AH

www.summerhillbooks.co.uk

email: summerhillbooks@yahoo.co.uk

ISBN: 978-1-906721-56-5

Contents

INTRODUCTION 5
ACKNOWLEGEMENTS 6
& SOURCES OF REFERENCE

PLACES OF WORSHIP
Monkseaton Methodist Church 7
The Wesleyan Chapel and Fairway Hall 9
St Andrew's Church 10
St John's Church 11
St Mary's Church 12
St Peter's Church 14

THE RAILWAY SYSTEM
BrierDene Station 16
Monkseaton Station 18
West Monkseaton Station 23

SCHOOLS AND EDUCATION
Langley Avenue School 25
Monkseaton Community High School 27
Monkseaton Village Schools 27
Monkseaton West County Primary School 29
Valley Gardens Secondary Modern School 30
Whitley Bay High School 31

PEOPLE AND LEISURE
Bobby Thompson 32
Robert Davison 35
William Weaver Tomlinson 42
Monkseaton Morrismen 49
Monkseaton Cricket Club 52
Whitley Bay Football Club 54
Whitley Bay Ice Rink 56
Red House Farm Allotment Society 57

CRIME
The Hillheads Murders 58
The Monkseaton Shootings 60

HILLHEADS
Hill Heads Overview 62
Hill Heads Slaughterhouse 64
West Park 65
Marden Quary 67

MISCELLANEOUS
Monkseaton Air Raids 70
Monkseaton Directories 74
Sewer Gas Lamps 86
Hidden Monkseaton 87
Royal Visit to Monkseaton 90
Monkseaton Memories 91

IMPORTANT INSTITUTION, AT MONK-SEATON, NEAR NORTH SHIELDS.

To the Worshipful the Magistrates of the East Division of Castle Ward, resident in Whitley.

GENTLEMEN, We, the Undersigned, respectfully request you to Call a PUBLIC MEETING of the inhabitants of Monkseaton, Whitley and the adjoining Townships, for the purpose of Forming an Institution for the Moral and Intellectual Improvement of the people, but especially the Young Men connected with those Places.

Wm. Davison	Thos Lowrie
Joseph Nixon	John Hall
Robert Miller	John Fenwick
Edwd. Brown	George Davidson
John Duxfield	Stephen House
Fenwick Aynsley	John Cleasby
Joseph Burnett	Wm. Love
Henry Dunn	Thomas Bell
J. Fenwick (Rake House)	Robt. Brown
William Nixon	James Hall
Henry Nicholson	John Young
John Moor	Luke Mason
Edwd. Collingwood	Robert Thompson
John Wright	Jas. Davidson
Wm. Atkinson	Geo. Ramsey
Joseph Dunn	T. Harbutt
Henry Whitfield	

In compliance with the above Requisition, we hereby appoint a MEETING of the inhabitants of Monkseaton, Whitley and adjoining Townships, on TUESDAY, the 8th December next, at the house of Mr. JOHN DUXFIELD, Ship Inn, Monkseaton, at Six in the Evening.

HENRY MITCALFE.
J.H. FRYER.

Whitley, Nov.30, 1810.

INTRODUCTION

Despite the rumours, I have never professed to be an expert on Monkseaton Village and I still firmly hold that view, however I do believe that my interest, combined with years of study, backed up by a large collection of photographs and picture postcards has helped me develop a better knowledge and understanding of its background and its history.

With that in mind, I have compiled what I consider to be a fairly comprehensive history of the village, much of which has finally been brought together in two books – Monkseaton Village Volume One and Monkseaton Village Volume Two.

This book, Volume Two, therefore concludes the history of the Village from my perspective.

Neither of these books are intended to provide a complete history of the village. Their objective is simply to give a general overview in words and pictures of many of the most important aspects, past and present that we know of, or recognise in Monkseaton and its immediate surroundings.

Of course Monkseaton Village has seen many changes over the years, some of which we can remember and others which have long been lost in the mists of time.

From its origins as a medieval settlement in the 12th century to a farming community in the 1600s and beyond, the village has grown and expanded to become what it is today.

The core pattern of the village still exists and plenty evidence remains of its early history.

On 14th February 2006, Monkseaton Village was designated a Conservation Area which in theory will help to protect much of our past heritage for many years to come.

Combined with Volume One, I hope that the information in this book continues to prove a popular source of reference, and that you enjoy reading it.

Charlie Steel
Monkseaton,
November 2012

Members and scholars of the Monkseaton Wesleyan Sunday School, Chapel Lane, c.1910.

ACKNOWLEDGEMENTS

It is not possible to put a book together of this nature without the assistance of other people. Over a number of years, the people listed below have each made a significant contribution to the content of this publication, and it is therefore important that they are personally acknowledged by name:

ITEM	CONTRIBUTOR
Bobby Thompson	Keith Thompson
Hidden Monkseaton	Tom and Sue Tait
Hillheads Murders	Northumbria Police
Langley Avenue School	Val Brown
Monkseaton Brewery	Mike Sowter
Monkseaton Cricket Club	Tony Errington
Monkseaton Directories	Peter Hasselby
Monkseaton Methodist Church	Steve and Joyce Adamson
Monkseaton Morrismen	Bryan Jackson
	Steve Ellwood
Monkseaton Shootings	Northumbria Police,
	Pam, Debbie and Roger Mackintosh
Monkseaton Station	Chris Boylan
	Ken White
Monkseaton Village Schools	Brian and Pauline Swan
Monkseaton West Primary School	Jill Brown
St Andrew's Church	Ray and Ann Hammond
	Edith Corby
St John's Church	Ian Nicholson
St Peter's Church	Jan Porter
Whitley Bay Ice Rink	Francis Smith
	Kath Smith

Special thanks also go to all the staff of North Tyneside Local Studies Library for their patience and valued assistance as well as Andrew Clark for his valuable help, advice and support.

SOURCES OF REFERENCE

Many reference sources and publications have also been utilised in order to complete this publication, however some of the more significant ones include the following:

Ordnance Survey Mapping

North Shields Library – Local Studies Centre

Remembering the Past – Resourcing the Future	Kath Smith and all relevant contributors to the North Shields Library Club.
Historical Notes on Cullercoats, Whitley and Monkseaton	William Weaver Tomlinson.
Kellys Directories	Kellys Directories Ltd.
Wards Directories	R. Ward & Sons.
Monkseaton Conservation Area Character Appraisal	North Tyneside Council.
Wikipedia	Internet Based

PLACES OF WORSHIP
MONKSEATON METHODIST CHURCH

Monkseaton Methodist Church dates to around 1660. It was originally part of Village Farm, and formed the turnip house, byres barns and stables.

The structure first came into use as a place of worship during 1899 when it was purchased by local dignitary and benefactor; Col. T.W. Elliott, of Monkseaton Cottage, who converted the building into a little church for use by the Anglicans. The chapel was entrusted to the care of the Reverend G.M.J. Bailey.

Often referred to as the 'Mission House', Col. Elliott presented two cannons to the church soon after it opened, and which remained in place at the front of the building until 1942, when they were removed in a salvage drive for the war effort.

It was due to the presence of these cannons, that for many years the church was often referred to as the 'Gun Chapel'. These cannons once formed part of the ordinance of Scarborough Castle.

The church itself had an adjoining hall which opened on 21st December 1906 to become known as the Monkseaton Village Room which was used for concerts, lectures and non-sectarian events to benefit the moral and social well-being of the area.

In 1913, the Anglicans left the building to move into their new church in Claremont Road (St Mary's). The 'Gun Chapel' was immediately taken over by the Wesleyans who had moved from Chapel Lane during this year, and on 12th May 1913, in an opening ceremony, the keys were formally handed over to the Wesleyans. A celebratory meeting was held in the evening where many of the local churches on the circuit were represented.

In 1914, at the outbreak of the First World War, the military authorities requisitioned the church premises

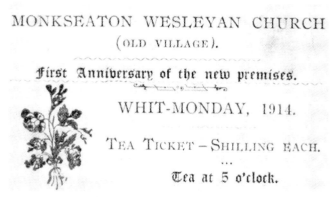

A tea ticket for Whit Monday, 1914.

which were used as a billet for troops of the 3rd Battalion West Yorkshire Regiment, during which time the Wesleyans temporarily returned to the former chapel in Chapel Lane for their services throughout the duration of the war.

The church later became better known as Monkseaton Methodist Church and still exists with a strong congregation.

At a ceremony held at the church on 12th May 1913, Alderman John Robert Hogg JP (centre) accepts the keys for the new church, from Col. T.W. Elliott on behalf of the Wesleyans

Inside the newly opened Church – May 1913.

A 1920s bicycle outing of the Church Mission Band to help spread the word of the Lord.

THE WESLEYAN CHAPEL AND FAIRWAY HALL

This small stone building stood on Chapel Lane opposite South West Farm Stackyard, and has already been covered in Volume One. However, the adjoining building, known as 'Fairway Hall' stood close by, on the site of the present clinic. For many years it was known as 'The Tin Chapel' because the wooden framework of which it was built was protected by corrugated metal sheeting.

Annexed to the Wesleyan Chapel, this building was used for many years as a community or village hall until its destruction on 29th August 1940 after taking a direct hit in a bombing raid over Monkseaton.

Above: Looking north on Chapel Lane, c.1930, showing the Old Wesleyan Chapel.

Left: Chapel Lane, c.1925, showing the entrance gate and 'The Tin Chapel' (Fairway Hall).

ST ANDREW'S CHURCH

The history of St Andrew's Church in Monkseaton goes back to 1928, when a site on the corner of Eastfield Avenue and Woodleigh Road was secured by the Presbyterian Church of England at a cost of £955 on which to accommodate the new building and in 1932 St Andrews was established. Preaching began and services were held in Monkseaton Village Primary School, on Chapel Lane.

The first stage of building work commenced in February 1933 with construction of the Church Hall, which was completed in less than 5 months. The total cost of this part of the work including furnishings was £2,862.

On Wednesday 28th June 1933 the Church Hall was officially opened by a Mr. J. Saunders with the Reverend Gladstone Hughes M.A. of the Presbyterian Church of New Zealand accepting the temporary pastorate.

Rev. Hughes conducted services until September 1934 when the first minister, the Reverend H. Burns-Jamieson M.A. was ordained and inducted. He became an army chaplain in September 1939.

It was proposed that the actual Church would be built at a later stage when finances were available; however during Christmas 1937, the building fund received a boost when an anonymous member donated the sum of £2,000 towards the construction costs of the new church.

On 12th June 1939 building work eventually began, with foundation stones being laid on 22nd July by the Reverend J.M. Richardson and Mr J. Hall Forster. It was fortunate that the outbreak of th Second World War less than two months later did not unduly delay any building work as a majority of the materials had already been delivered to the site.

The church was designed on very simple lines, aiming at quiet dignity in its proportions. Consisting of a chancel and nave with central and side aisles along with the adjoining vestibules and secondary rooms.

The nave slopes gently towards the chancel, and the versatility of chairs was given preference over fixed pews.

Windows were designed to be out of

St Andrew's Church, 1957.

the direct view of the congregation, whilst consideration was given to the lighting of the chancel by both natural and artificial illumination.

Externally, the building is faced with rustic bricks and a slate roof with a small internal court or cloister being formed between the church and the adjoining church hall. (This area has since been replaced by the new extension work of 2009.)

By 1941, construction of the new church was complete, and on 22nd February, St Andrew's Church was officially opened by Mr and Mrs J. Hall Forster. The seating accommodation in the church comprised 300 seats in the nave and 30 in the choir.

Following the resignation of Reverend Jamieson, it was in December of this year that Reverend William Louttit took over the services until July 1946 when he was succeeded by the Reverend Alfred Webb B.A., the longest serving incumbent who remained with St. Andrew's for a period of 28 years until his retirement in 1974, during which time the Presbyterian Church of England became part of the United Reformed Church (1972).

Subsequent incumbents have included; Reverend Tom E. Grant (1974-1992), Reverend G. Trevor Holborn (1993-1997), Reverend Gordon Connacher (1999-2007), Reverend Dr. David Peel (2009).

In 1950, a memorial stained glass window was unveiled in the church to the memory of those who fell in the Second World War. The artist and designer, Mr. L.C. Evetts depicted St Andrew, who, with his left hand, is drawing a net of fish from the sea, whilst his right hand is raised to denote the martyrdom he suffered symbolised by the saltire cross at the head of the window.

The saint stands upon his native heath, in which the blueberry plant is introduced. The symbols of the burning bush and open bible are represented at either side of the figure. At the bottom corners, sea plants form a decorative finish. The technique was devised to admit the greatest amount of light and colour to the church.

The church has been going strong ever since, and has served the community of Monkseaton well, and currently has a strong and lively worshipping congregation. The latest phase of building work which was completed in 2009, included alterations to the front of the building which incorporated a new porch and entrance.

Many organisations which have at one time met, or continue to meet at the church include a Ladies Guild, Scouts and Guides, Dance Groups and a Gilbert and Sullivan Society and is still a popular venue for concerts and a variety of community events.

ST JOHN'S CHURCH

During the 19th century the separate sections of Methodism spread, and at by the beginning of the 1900s, Wesleyan, Primitive and United Methodist Churches existed in Whitley Bay as well as a Wesleyan Methodist Church in Monkseaton.

In 1909 it was agreed that there was a need for an additional Wesleyan Church to cater for the increasing population and accordingly, a site consisting of 2,000 square yards at the corner of Ilfracombe Gardens and Balmoral Gardens was purchased at a cost of £900.

Building work commenced on what was to be a temporary wooden structure, capable of seating a congregation of around 300 people.

Furnishings including lighting, heating, lavatories and railings around the site totalled £130, and on 1st December that year in the presence of a large gathering, the church was opened by a Miss Ogilvie and her brother; Mr Frank Ogilvie of North Shields.

Almost immediately, a building fund was established in order to finance the erection of a permanent building, but the First World War delayed progress, and the decision to proceed was not taken until the early 1920s.

This decision was stimulated by a pledge of £5,000 from Sir Arthur Munro Sutherland, a distinguished Tyneside industrialist and philanthropist, on the proviso that the church opened free of debt, and ultimately this condition was met.

The architects for the new church were Marshall and Tweedy of Newcastle and the contractor was William Hall of Gateshead, who also manufactured all the interior fittings including the oak pews, choir stalls, communion table and pulpit.

The foundation stone was laid on 9th May 1925 by Sir Arthur

OPENING AND DEDICATION of
St. John's Wesleyan Methodist Church, Monkseaton,
TO-DAY, SATURDAY, FEBRUARY 20th, 1926.
DOOR OPENED at 3 p.m. by—
Sir ARTHUR SUTHERLAND, Bart., K.B.E.
DEDICATION SERVICE following, conducted by—
Rev. R. A. MITCHESON BROWN and Rev. H. M. BLEBY, B.A.
TEA at 4.45 p.m.   Tickets One Shilling each
PUBLIC MEETING AT 6.30 p.m.
Chairman—Ald. R. MASON, J.P., supported by Sir ARTHUR SUTHERLAND, Bart., K.B.E., Rev. THOS. KIRKUP, of London; Local Clergy and Ministers, and Circuit Ministers.

SUNDAY, FEBRUARY 21st, 1926.
MORNING SERVICE at 10.45 a.m., at which the Chairman and Urban District Council will be present.
YOUNG PEOPLE'S RALLY at 3 p.m. Chairman—Mr. Geo. Potts.
EVENING SERVICE at 6.30 p.m.
Preacher at all Services:
REV. THOS. KIRKUP, of London (Secretary of the Conference).

Sutherland and building work was completed within a year. The new church opened on Saturday 20th February 1926 at a total cost of £15,000.

The first sermon was preached by Rev. R.A.M. Brown, chairman of the Newcastle district, and so began a future of worship at St John's Church.

Following a deed of union in 1932, the church became known as the Methodist Church of St John. The original 'temporary' building was redesignated as the 'Wesley Hall' which survived until the early 1960s before it was demolished to make way for the present new Wesley Hall.

This new building was opened on 18th September 1965 at a cost of £26,000 by Mr. W.E. Guest, who at that time was one of the oldest church members.

Past Ministers at St John's have included:

1926	Rev. G. Kellet Grice
1928	Rev. Lounce Wood
1931	Rev. Walter J. Bull
1932	Rev. Lounce Wood
1933	Rev. Albert Antcliff
1934	Rev, A.J. Howitt
1936	Rev. J.W. Grindell
1941	Rev. H. Mortimer
1948	Rev. Robert Flenley
1953	Rev. G. Selby Bell
1959	Rev. Arthur H. Jex
1968	Rev. Wilfred Hayes
1978	Rev. G. Rushton
1983	Rev. K. Finch
1987	Rev. A. Temple
1995	Rev. K. Harbour
2000	Rev. P. Cleever-Thorpe
2009	Rev. C.S. Hall

St John's Church, 2011.

ST MARY'S CHURCH

St Paul's Parish once covered the part of Whitley and Monkseaton now known as the Parish of St Mary.

In the early 1900s, there were very few houses in that part of Monkseaton and as the district began to develop as a residential area, plans were made to establish a church.

The interior of St Mary's Church Hall, dressed for the 1914 Harvest Festival.

As a result, on 23rd May 1911, a submission was made to the Local Authority Buildings Committee to erect a temporary Church Hall on a site in Claremont Gardens, which would be known as St Mary's.

The hall was quickly built and opened in September of the same year. It was served by a series of Curates-in-Charge and by February 1920, St Mary's had been established in its own right as a separate Parish.

Soon afterwards, the congregation were eager to go ahead with the construction of a permanent church and in 1921, plans were drawn up and finalised in 1928.

The architects were Wood and Oakley, and the building contractors were Messrs. John Jackson and Sons of Newcastle.

Construction work commenced soon afterwards with the foundation stone being laid on 9th May 1931 by the Bishop of the Diocese.

The church was designed to incorporate a bell-tower towards the north west corner, however this was never built. The building costs at this time were over £8,000

The old church hall still remained, and during the war years, was requisitioned to accommodate troops and so many of the social and fundraising activities were temporarily suspended.

By 1957, the hall had reached the end of its useful life and was demolished to make way for the present hall which was rebuilt on the same site adjoining the south side of the church and opening in 1959.

Laying the Foundation Stone of the new church, 9th May 1931.

Over the years, St Mary's Church has been home to many organisations including a Mothers' Union group and Girl Guide association first established in the 1920s.

The church and hall are still used for many community based events and activities.

The Roll of clergy between 1904-1928 included; C.L. Gwilliam, G.H.J. Bailey, C.R. Liversey and E. Fletcher.

The subsequent incumbents were:

1928-1936	Rev. W.E. Hicks	1975-1982	Rev. D. Smith
1936-1938	Rev. J.M. Nicholson	1983-1990	Rev. J.M. Lowen
1938-1951	Rev. S. Thistlewood	1990-1999	Rev. J.L. Hallatt
1951-1960	Rev. A. Wilson	2000-2004	Rev. Dr. C.H. Knights
1961-1967	Rev. H.I. Jones	2005-	Rev. Canon Dr. R.P. Greenwood
1968-1975	Rev. C. Turnbull		

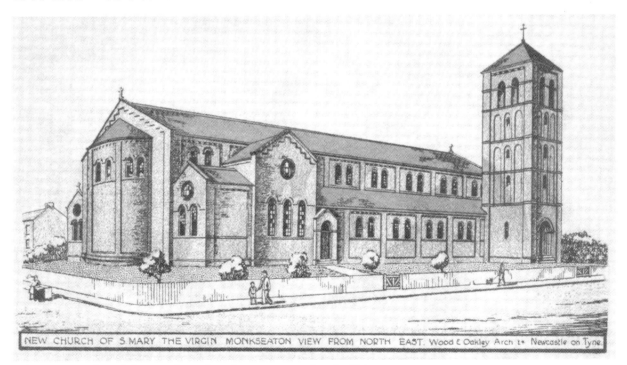

NEW CHURCH OF S.MARY THE VIRGIN MONKSEATON VIEW FROM NORTH EAST. Wood & Oakley Arch ts Newcastle on Tyne.

The original architects drawing incorporated a bell-tower.

ST PETER'S CHURCH

Records indicate that in 1886 Monkseaton Cottage (58 Front Street) was used for Church of England Services which were usually led by visiting clergy from St Paul's at Whitley.

The origins of St Peter's Church in Monkseaton originally began at what is now the Methodist Chapel opposite the Black Horse on Front Street in the early 1900s, however when the building reverted back to the Methodists, St. Peter's acquired two old Army huts on nearby Chapel Lane and moved there until such time as funding allowed the erection of a permanent building. The premises became known as 'The Tin Chapel' because the huts were made from wood which in turn were encased in corrugated iron for strength and protection.

Over the years, fundraising efforts took place for a new Church of St Peter to be built nearby, and the original proposal was that the building would be erected between Chapel Lane and the back of the present houses at the end of Closefield Grove, however these plans were abandoned when a more centralised site was secured on the corner of the present Woodleigh and Elmwood Road.

With a grant from the Bishop's Church Extension Fund, the land was purchased in 1937 for £2,000 from John Robert Hogg, a North Shields leather merchant and building work commenced soon afterwards.

St Peter's Church, 2006.

The church was designed by a Mr George Holmes of Tynemouth and built by the Monkseaton firm of R.A. Gofton and Sons at cost price, which equated to a gift of over £2000. The entire structure is cruciform in shape and was built on a concrete raft to give it the same strength as many medieval churches. The finished church had seating accommodation for over 400 people.

Building work was completed in 1938, and the church was consecrated by the Rt Revd. Harold Bilbrough, Lord Bishop of Newcastle on the vigil of St Peter, at 7.30pm on Tuesday 28th June 1938.

In October 1939, the Church Commissioners met to arrange the boundaries and declared St Peter's as a separate parish. It was not until 1940 that the church received its first curate; the Reverend George Earle.

On 29th August 1940 during an air raid over Monkseaton, a bomb fell close to the church causing some structural damage and blowing out many of the windows. Blackout material was used to cover them and they remained that way until the end of the war years before being replaced with new glass.

The vestry however was completely destroyed and not rebuilt until after the war. The church and Lady Chapel were partly affected and apparently, during the blackout days, evensong was held in the afternoons.

Ironically, during the same air raid, a bomb also fell on Chapel Lane, completely destroying the former tin buildings which once housed St Peter's Church

In 1951, a proposal recommended that a new window of three lights should be placed at the east end of the church as a war memorial, and

Bomb damage to St Peter's Church, August 1940.

when eventually completed in 1955, was dedicated as such on the Remembrance Sunday of that year.

In the meantime 1954 had seen further building work commence on the new adjoining church hall, better known to many as the Cross Keys Community Hall which is the home to many local groups and clubs and is regularly used for various local activities and functions.

The Clergy of St Peter through its life have included the following incumbents and Curates;

Incumbents:

1938-49	Revd. H.S.S. Jackson	1969-89	Revd. C. White
1949-56	Revd. L. Watson	1989-96	Revd P. Dunlop
1956-59	Revd L.D. Blathwayt	1996-2011	Revd. Canon J.A. Robertson
1960-68	Revd. G. Bateson	2011 -	Revd. J. Wood

Curates:

1941-45	Revd. G.H. Earle	1972-74	Revd. J.A. Pyle
1949-51	Revd. P. Taylor	1975-78	Revd. J.A. Robertson
1954-56	Revd. A. Gray	1990-92	Revd. N. Wilson
1957-59	Revd. C.J.D. Rogerson	1992-95	Revd. P. Barron
1962-65	Revd. H. Myers	1997-2001	Revd A. Bowden
1965-68	Revd. P. Lister	2002-05	Revd A. Elder
1966-69	Revd. W.J. Hatchley	2005-08	Revd L. Gardham
1969-72	Revd. L.M. Bate	2008 -	Revd P.A. Craighead

An inverted cross is often considered to be a sign of satanic desecration of the most sacred symbol of the Christian faith. To turn the cross upside down is believed, to be a sign of inverted or reversed grace, but to many Christians it is believed to be representative of St Peter's devotion to his Lord and Saviour.

When Peter was martyred for his faith he asked to be crucified upside down because he did not feel that he was worthy to die as his master did, upright.

St Peter's cross is therefore a symbol of humility before God and trusting in his saving grace even in the face of a cruel death at the hands of your enemies.

St Peter's Cross is often depicted with a set of keys being representative of the keys of the kingdom of heaven that Christian tradition holds were entrusted to Peter before the death and resurrection of Jesus Christ.

THE RAILWAY SYSTEM
BRIERDENE STATION

By 1910 the Tyneside Electric passenger service was well established. Traffic to the coastal railway stations at Tynemouth, Cullercoats, Whitley and Monkseaton was steadily increasing and with rapid housing development taking place at these localities, the idea of building a new community at Seaton Sluice, halfway along the coast between Monkseaton and Blyth began to take shape.

The landowner; Lord Hastings was to convey 21 acres of land to the railway company to allow for the construction of a new branch line which commenced in 1913, and it was estimated that work would be complete and the line ready for opening by November 1914.

The contract for the proposed line was awarded to C.M. Skinner, and the route which became known as the Collywell Bay Branch began from a spur on the existing Blyth and Tyne Avenue Branch (called BrierDene Junction) which was about one mile north of Monkseaton Station and situated near the end of where Woodburn Square is now built. The line then curved east behind BrierDene Farm and ran along the western edge of what is now Whitley Bay Golf Course.

An intermediate station with a passing loop at BrierDene was built, additional to which it was intended that the Avenue Branch line, as far as BrierDene Junction was to be changed from single to double track and electrified.

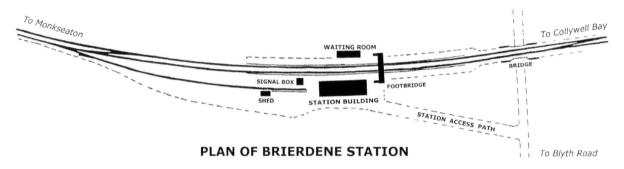

PLAN OF BRIERDENE STATION

The actual station buildings and platforms were situated behind Whitley Bay Cemetery and Crematorium and accessed by a pathway on Blyth Road, diagonally opposite the present caravan site. The site has now been grassed over and forms part of the golf course, however ruins of the nearby stone bridge abutments are still evident.

BrierDene Station looking south towards Monkseaton, 1930. (Note the absence of track by the east platform). The lattice footbridge was originally situated at the old Monkseaton Station and later moved to BrierDene.

The station buildings were designed as elaborate timber structures rather than of brick or stone materials with an estimated building cost of £1,226.

By 1914, construction of the branch line and stations was well under way and almost complete; however at the outbreak of the First World War, work was suspended for an indefinite period.

The work which had already been carried out at that time included the laying out of around 4 miles of track, along with all the necessary platforms, bridges and signal boxes at a total expenditure of £28,592.

Because the Collywell Bay line had never been fully completed and physically opened to rail traffic, it did not become a railway that was entitled to any wartime compensation from the government, however before the end of 1917, a further 1 mile of track was laid down in order to serve some nearby gun emplacements as part of the coastal defence system.

The scheme was reviewed in 1924 when it was estimated that it would cost over £50,000 to rehabilitate the branch, as a result of which, much of the the track and stations at BrierDene and Collywell Bay lay abandoned throughout the 1920s.

Partially dismantled, the remains of the old stone bridge is now the only evidence left of the old railway connecting the nearby BrierDene Station.

In 1930, Thomas Hornsby, the Divisional General Manager of the railway company (LNER) estimated that a half hourly passenger and goods service based on the carriage of 280 passengers per day at a fare of 3d each, would generate an income of less than £2,000 per year and concluded that combined with the high cost of reinstatement work, the line would not be economically viable. He therefore submitted a memorandum, proposing the abandonment of this branch.

Accordingly, Lord Hastings released the LNER from their initial obligation to purchase the land, but this was subject to removing rails and bridge superstructures, and leaving the fences on each side of the line intact. Because of the high cost of recovery of the stone platforms and buildings, these remained in situ, and all other necessary abandonment work had been undertaken by the end of 1932.

The route of the old line is still easily traceable for practically all of its length apart from the section near Collywell Bay, which has since disappeared under new housing development at Old Hartley.

The original embankment and path of the old railway is still clearly visible, part of which runs parallel to Blyth Road between Whitley Cemetery and Old Hartley.

Map showing the route of the Collywell Bay branch line and the location of Brierdene Station.
The map is for illustrative purposes only as many of the streets shown had not been laid out at the time.

MONKSEATON STATION

In 1852, the Blyth and Tyne Railway became a public company, established to develop rail transport in North Tyneside.

Not to be confused with the present Monkseaton Station of 1915, the original Monkseaton Station was a much smaller building situated east of the present structure, and stood slightly to the north of Osborne Gardens on the site of the present Medical Centre.

Consisting of two short platforms, waiting rooms and a signal box, it was built in 1859, and opened on 31st October 1860. A gated level crossing took the tracks across Marine Avenue into what is now the entrance to Churchill Playing Fields.

Looking south over the level crossing on Marine Avenue, the original Monkseaton Station buildings are situated to the right, and the signal box on the left is where the present Monkseaton Medical Centre is now sited. The houses on Osborne Gardens are hidden beyond. The footbridge in the distance was later removed and transferred to BrierDene Station.

During the 1800s, much of the life in the village centred around the station which was considered to be of some importance.

The early station had a comfortable waiting room and verandah, and was the pick of the stations on the Blyth and Tyne Railway. The general manager, Mr Joseph Cabrey was very proud of it.

The station served as a common meeting ground, where during the summer, people occupied the platform seats for hours on end. The signal box was a select sort of club, frequented by the privileged. It served as a reading, debating and hairdressing room for passengers, and cabs plied regularly between Monkseaton and Whitley.

A notice on the wooden refreshment stall owned by a Mr Peter Rolls displayed the royal cipher: V.R., which was only possible because the proprietor had previously been in business serving some of Queen Victoria's barracks.

There were few trains per day, and they were scarcely on time, and rumour has it that it was possible for a person to leave the train to walk into Monkseaton on the understanding that the train would wait for him!

When wells and springs ran dry in the summertime, a supply of water could always be obtained from the station.

Quantities of the famous beer from Monkseaton

The First Monkseaton Railway Station stood adjacent to Osborne Gardens.

Brewery would be loaded up at the station each week, and it was part of the arrangement that a bucketful of ale would be sent for the benefit of the staff. Needless to say, there were always several people who managed to drop by for a few minutes rest at the opportune moment. John Donovan was a very popular station master who died in 1886. He was succeeded by a Mr F.W. Guy who recalled the staff when he took over comprised; one clerk, two porters, and two signalmen, and sometimes not enough income at the station was available to pay their wages.

Prior to the installation of gas lights, there were a dozen oil lamps which used sperm whale oil. Every time a strong wind blew, the lamps would go out. Great fires were always kept well lit in the waiting rooms where people could meet to talk and socialise.

The station was renamed as Monkseaton on 3rd July 1882 when the new station at Whitley Bay opened. This soon put an end to all the old frolics and horseplay. The cabs ceased to ply, Peter Roll's establishment closed down, and the 'select' club at the signal box was abandoned after the installation of a new signalling system.

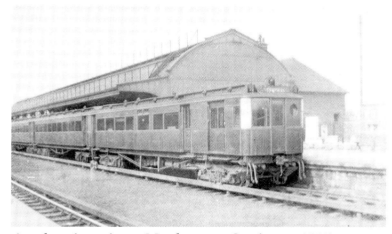

An electric train at Monkseaton Station, c.1915.

Earlier, in 1861, the Blyth and Tyne Railway Company had acquired the abandoned waggonway which ran between Monkseaton and Tynemouth, and laid a line of rails to connect the two villages. (This waggonway roughly followed a straight line to the west of the Broadway.)

Building on the route of the old waggonway, the railway from Monkseaton ran towards Hillheads Road, behind what is now Kingsley Avenue, to a point almost opposite the present Lovaine Avenue, which in 1861, enabled passengers to board the new railway for Newcastle at a halt called Whitley Hillheads next to the Railway Inn.

In 1882, when the railway was realigned to include Whitley and Cullercoats, the site became a goods station and marshalling yard, and the old line was closed.

The long sidings dealt with considerable quantities of domestic coal, and the area provided facilities as a lay-over line for the steam train that ran from Monkseaton to Blyth on the Avenue branch, as well as parking facilities for overnight stabling of electric and off peak daytime trains..

To the west of Lovaine Avenue, evidence of the old track is still visible where it once ran through the former council yard, across Hotspur Avenue, over the rugby field, past the western edge of Marden Quarry and skirted Shaftesbury Crescent, where a slight embankment remains.

By 1899, approximately 64 trains per day entered and left Monkseaton Station, including 22 express trains. About 22 trains ran to and from the station on Sundays.

In July 1915, the old station closed after the construction of the present Monkseaton Station, where the railway track, including part of the 'Avenue Branch' line were re-aligned and moved further west, to where the new station was built, at the junction with Norham

Road. This development also incorporated the construction of the present road bridge leading from Front Street to Marine Avenue.

Hartley Avenue was laid out following the realignment of the railway, and shadowed the arc of the newly realigned 'Avenue Branch' line to Blyth. (Axed by Dr Richard Beeching on 2nd November 1964.)

It was referred to as the 'Avenue Branch' because it crossed over the 'Avenue', just west of Seaton Delaval Hall prior to reaching Hartley Station, and hence the name of

Monkseaton Station interior, c.1935.

Hartley Avenue was derived from here. This former railway track is now a pathway and nature trail running behind the houses on the west side of Hartley Avenue.

As the railway at Monkseaton developed, the district became a popular residential area for those businessmen whose offices were located in Newcastle, and with a journey time of less than half an hour, the dream of being able to live close to the coast was realised.

By 1953, Monkseaton Station was still a busy stop on the Coast line, and provided access to the sea for much of Tyneside's population, with a frequent train service running through.

Eight grassed lawns and gardens were situated in the wide gap between the up and down platforms, which were well tended by the staff. This was a feature believed to be unique in the country.

At this time, the station was overseen by 5 principal staff members, (*right, from top to bottom*); Mr J. Calder, Stationmaster, who also supervised West Monkseaton and Whitley Bay, George Halbert (Station Foreman), Mrs Elsie Sanderson (Clerk), Harry Ferguson (Ticket Collector) and Frank Appleby (Porter).

Following demolition of the old Monkseaton station, discussions were held by Whitley Council and the North Eastern Railway Company to purchase the land, which was successfully acquired in 1922.

Using unemployed labour, the area was laid out as a recreation park with facilities for Tennis Courts and Bowling Greens. Councillor C.W. Souter, whose home in Osborne Gardens overlooked the old railway station, led these negotiations, and Souter Park was appropriately named in his honour.

The new Monkseaton Station became an important stop on the Newcastle-Coast loop line, and had many facilities which included left luggage, goods and parcel offices, a rail booking office, waiting rooms with seating and coal fires, as well as all the usual platform kiosks and facilities usually seen at larger stations.

By the 1920s and 1930s, thousands of holidaymakers and day-trippers would flock to the coast from Newcastle and its suburbs, as it was just a short walk down Marine Avenue to the seaside for those who wished to avoid Whitley Bay Centre. By the end of the Second World War, Monkseaton station was increasingly used by commuters travelling to and from Newcastle.

In 1979, the loop line and all associated stations, including Monkseaton were taken over to become part of the present Tyne and Wear Metro System, and this service began to operate from 11th August 1980.

A typical scene as crowds of commuters wait on the west platform of Monkseaton Station, July 1957.

Monkseaton Railway Accidents

Two accidents of note have been recorded at Monkseaton Station over the years. The first of these occurred close to the original 1859 Station where the track crossed Marine Avenue and curved to the left continuing the loop back towards Newcastle however a spur controlled by points from the nearby signal box ran straight ahead to allow trains to either enter the sidings or join the old Avenue Branch Line.

On a foggy evening, just before 6pm on 1st January 1900 a tank engine with ten coaches pulled into the up platform. This train was the scheduled 5.47pm train from Newcastle Central (via Tynemouth) to New Bridge Street, which was running late. After a few moments, the train was given the signal to restart. As the driver had slightly overshot the signals when he brought the train to a stop, he was unable to see the signal clearly when he set off again.

Because of its late arrival, the signalman wrongly thought that this was actually the 5.58pm arrival from Newcastle which was scheduled to terminate at Monkseaton Sidings at this time, and had set his points accordingly, however when the train pulled away, he realised his mistake having sent the train on the wrong track where it collided with the buffer stops in the sidings at a speed of around 20mph. The train ran on for a further 25 yards before coming to a halt. No serious injuries were reported.

A second accident of note occurred at Monkseaton Station at 9.10am on Saturday 13th October 1956 when a goods train, consisting of a steam locomotive and coal tender, drawing a total of 22 wagons loaded with steel plates on the down line from the direction of West Monkseaton was passing under Front Street Road Bridge.

The fast moving locomotive approached the station, tender first when the bogie wheels jumped the tracks causing the engine and the first five of its wagons to derail and overturn. The ensuing impact caused the locomotive to impact with the end of the northern section of platform, tearing up huge coping stones, ripping up railway lines and demolishing a large

Monkseaton Station, c.1955.

signal gantry.

The driver was a Mr. Jack Stacey of Walkergate who was trapped in the resultant wreckage until his rescue was effected shortly afterwards. Mr Stacey lost consciousness after suffering a broken leg, cuts, bruises and burns from the steam box and after being freed, was taken to Tynemouth Infirmary for treatment.

Overnight recovery of the damaged locomotive.

The remaining crew of the train; a fireman and a trainee driver managed to escape uninjured, however the guard suffered minor injuries. Passengers and commuters who were innocently waiting for their usual service trains on the adjacent platforms witnessed the accident were covered in steam, dust and debris as the huge engine shuddered to a halt nearby, but luckily no other injuries were caused.

It was only by good fortune that a passenger train which was due to arrive at Monkseaton at this time on the opposing (up) line, had been delayed at Tynemouth, otherwise the incident may have been much more serious had the train been running to schedule. Emergency rescue and maintenance crews with heavy lifting gear were quickly called out from Gateshead and Darlington to clear the wreckage.

Railway track in both directions suffered significant damage and although salvage and removal work began later that day, it took many hours to clear the site and inspect the resulting damage which took until after midnight the following day for the site to be cleared.

Significant damage was caused to the track and East platform.

Major repair work to the damaged section of railway track and platform began on Monday 15th October and emergency bus links were set up to ferry passengers between Backworth and Whitley Bay stations whilst new track, foundations and ballast were laid. An investigation which followed the incident, found that the cause of the derailment was due to a broken axle on the tender of the locomotive. No blame was attributable to the driver or crew. After recovery, it was turned upright, and along with the tender was covered with tarpaulins and moved to nearby sidings where it remained for almost a week. The locomotive itself was a class J27 No. 65794, built at Darlington in 1906. The salvage was later towed to the British Railways Darlington Works where over a period of five weeks, it was stripped down, overhauled and rebuilt with a reconditioned tender.

The locomotive then came back into service, looking very smart with nothing to suggest that it had been involved in a major accident, and following two further overhauls, gave another nine years service before eventually being scrapped in June 1965.

WEST MONKSEATON STATION

West Monkseaton Railway Station was built by the London and North Eastern Railway Company, specifically to cater for the new housing that was currently being built nearby.

The actual construction work took just over a month, and the station opened to the public for the first time on 20th March 1933. Both platforms and a majority of the station buildings were manufactured from concrete and wood, with the exterior being a good example of Art Deco design.

West Monkseaton Station was designed to incorporate retail kiosks. Finlay & Co. Ltd were tobacconists and W.H. Smith and Son were newsagents and stationers.

Looking onto the wooden platforms of West Monkseaton Station, in 1933, it is apparent that some of the houses on Brantwood Avenue have not yet been built. In the distance, two parallel bridges crossed the railway lines towards Uplands, one of which was situated at the bottom of Brantwood Avenue and the other, just a few yards to the east on West Avenue. The Brantwood Avenue bridge was demolished in the early 1960s, but the second one on West Avenue still remains.

The station was built on the existing section of railway line adjacent to the bridge on Earsdon Road which was often referred to as 'Dickies Holm Bridge'. This was a narrow bridge crossing the railway lines on Earsdon Road which was widened in 1961 to accommodate the growing increase in road traffic.

West Monkseaton Station closed down on 10th September 1979 for eleven months whilst improvement work was carried out for the new Metro system. The station reopened on 11th August 1980 and remains an important commuter link in the system.

Earsdon Road, looking North in 1961. Travelling north towards the station, Earsdon Road originally took a slight right curve at the apex of the bridge. The station frontage therefore ran parallel to the line of the old road and this is evident by the photograph shown on page 23. When the bridge was widened and the road straightened, the station frontage became significantly offset from the line of the present main road.

West Monkseaton Station platforms, c.1968.

SCHOOLS AND EDUCATION
LANGLEY AVENUE SCHOOL

Built in the early 1950s, the second post-war school to be built in Whitley Bay, was Langley Avenue County Primary School, which occupies an area of 10 acres of land, to the south of Cauldwell Avenue. The total building cost was £132,820, and had the capability to accommodate 560 children.

The school first opened its doors to pupils in September 1952, soon after completion of the building work. It was one of the most modern schools of its type in Northumberland, and was tastefully decorated in pastel shades of cream and green.

It was not until some 9 months later, on Tuesday 16th June 1953, that the official opening ceremony took place. The Clerk of Northumberland County Council, Mr E.P. Harvey, conducted it. It commenced at 2pm that day before an audience of 350 parents and some local civic dignitaries including the chairman of Whitley Bay Urban District Council, Councillor Roger M. Charlton, who proposed a vote of thanks, in which he stressed the need for more school playing fields for the town. Thirty children concluded the ceremony by playing tunes on their recorders, in which the parents and visitors joining in the singing.

The infants' section of the school was located nearest the Townsville Avenue side whilst the junior section was situated towards the Canberra Avenue side. The school dining hall was situated almost midway between the two backing on to Elmfield Gardens. Miss K. Poule was appointed as headmistress of the infants' section, and Mr Frank R. Bryson was appointed as headmaster of the junior section.

Headmaster Frank Bryson.

Some of the first teaching staff included:
Mr Eric Lambert, Mrs Watkins Mr Bagnall, Mr Johnson, Miss Speed, Mr Barlow, Mr Sutherland, Miss Forster Miss Skelley and Mr George Usher.

During the 1950s, there were four individually coloured 'House Teams' at the school which were named after rivers in the North East, namely Tyne (Red), Tweed (Blue), Wansbeck (Green) and Coquet (Yellow). These teams were of special significance at the annual school sports days.

Mr Bert Sheldon was the local 'Lollipop Man' to the school for many years. He covered a crossing point on Seatonville Road outside the Regal Cinema, and was always happy to involve himself in the Schools Road Safety lessons. Photo c.1961

Mr Frank Bryson remained as headmaster of the junior school, until 30th May 1966 when he died in office and a plaque to his memory is located at the western end of the school.

In later years, owing to changes in the educational system, the infants' section closed, and was converted to accommodate children with special needs and disabilities, to become Woodlawn School, however Langley Avenue School itself still exists and is now situated within the area of the original junior school.

Coaches wait on Elmfield Gardens as pupils from the Junior School prepare for a day trip to York, c.1961.

Above: Children enjoying a road safety lesson in the playground during early 1961.

Left: Langley Avenue Junior School Football Team, 1961-62. Back row: unknown, Tom Gowland, Malcolm Tune, unknown, Denis Wilson, unknown. Front row: unknown, Paul Dryden, Trevor Thompson, Philip Skinner, unknown.

MONKSEATON COMMUNITY HIGH SCHOOL

The first Monkseaton High School was built on the lands of Seatonville Farm during the early 1970s and demolished in 2011 following the opening of the replacement building. Construction work on the new school began in June 2008 and was completed in time for pupils to move into the building in October 2009. Built at a massive cost of £20 million, the New Monkseaton Community High School was an innovative creation designed for North Tyneside Council by Ian Lancastle-Smith of Devereaux – a company of North East based architects with building work carried out by Shepherd Construction. The design of the school and bright colouring of the roof wind-catchers caused much local controversy as it appears completely alien to the surrounding housing and fieldscape.

The ellipse shape of the school however is very efficient in terms of space and land usage. It is aerodynamic and is able to regulate seasonal heating and cooling. Thermal solar panels are incorporated to provide tempered hot water and a natural air ventilation system which use 'wind-catchers' incorporated into the school's roof control to maintain a temperate climate within the building. Internally, the design beyond the formal teaching spaces incorporates a number of learning areas for students to study independently and the light airy feeling created throughout the school is a revolutionary move away from traditional, 'institutional' school design. The school is a mixed, comprehensive school for 13-18 year olds capable of accommodating up to 900 students.

MONKSEATON VILLAGE SCHOOLS

Situated on the south side of Chapel Lane, Monkseaton Village Infants School was built in 1930 for Northumberland County Council. This was the first building of what was to become a larger school complex which in 1932 was extended to include Monkseaton County Modern Senior School on Vernon Drive.

Monkseaton County Modern Senior School in 1932.

The Senior School opened on 22nd August 1932 and was designed to accommodate up to 460 pupils over the age of 11 years. The first headteacher was a Mr. William H. Turnbull. The school has always been popularly known as 'Bygate', presumably because of its close proximity to Bygate Road.

After reorganisation of the education and school structure in 1973, it was renamed as Monkseaton Middle School and accommodated pupils aged between 9 and 13 years.

The infants' school eventually closed down, and the building was taken over to accommodate various Council and Social Services departments before being vacated for demolition in 2007 to accommodate Bygate Court sheltered housing development whilst the old school caretaker's house still remains close by on Chapel Lane.

Right: The Senior School Blazer Badge depicted an unknown creature with the motto: 'Suivez la Raison', the literal translation of which is: 'Follow Reason'

The boys' entrance – Monkseaton Senior School, 1932.

Bygate Teaching Staff in the School Hall, c.1961. Front row, left to right: Miss Russell, Miss Rutter, Miss Hagan, Mr Henry, Mr Gallon (Headmaster), Mrs Main, Mrs Pritchard, Mrs Salkeld, Mrs Duncan. Back row: Mr Doig, Mr English, Mr Dodds, Mr Watts, Mr Brough, Mrs Caldwell, Mr White, Mr Graham (Deputy Headmaster), Mr Martin, Mr.McLean, Mr Brammer.

MONKSEATON WEST COUNTY PRIMARY SCHOOL

Built by Hastie Burton of North Shields at a cost of over £38,000, Monkseaton West County Primary School was the first school to be completed after post war building in the North East of England.

Complimenting the newly constructed Seatonville Council Housing Estate, the school which took over a year to build is situated on Appletree Gardens, and surrounded by spacious playing fields.

The school had been built because of the raising of the school leaving age, and the ever increasing child population of the area. It was designed to accommodate 320 children and had dining rooms and a canteen (the first school in Whitley Bay to have these facilities).

The doors were opened for the first time at 9am on 2nd March 1949, with 384 pupils on the roll which was 54 above its original design capacity.

The official opening ceremony was performed by Professor Brian Stanley (Director of the Institute of Education at Durham University) on 11th May 1949 in the presence of several officials and dignitaries which included; Insp. H.M. Spink (Director of Education for Northumberland), Councillor Alf Walton (Chairman of Whitley Urban District Council) and Mrs Walton, County Councillor D.F. Whittle and Mrs Whittle, Mr T. Bertram (Chairman of the East Castle Ward Bench), County Councillor Mrs Mary Allan, Councillor C.W. Williamson, Mr A.S. Ruddock (Clerk to Whitley Urban District Council), Mr W.W. Tasker (County Architect), Mr Albert Ford (Headmaster), and Mr John Baglee.

At this time, this school was one of the most modern and up to date of its type in the North, and at the opening ceremony, many visitors and pupils were unable to get into the large assembly hall and had to listen to the proceedings in the classrooms and passages whilst they were relayed throughout the school premises.

Mr Albert Ford, who came from Rockcliffe Junior School in Whitley Bay, was the first headmaster and his teaching staff were appointed as follows:

Class 1.	Mr G. Rowe
Class 2.	Mr G.A. Pougher
Class 3.	Miss L. Peace
Class 4.	Mrs G.A. Stevenson
Class 5.	Mrs J.M. Walker
Class 6.	Miss E.M. Brown
Class 7.	Miss G.L. Taylor
Class 8.	Miss J. Grey
Class 9.	Mrs M. Dunn
Class 10.	Mrs H.M. Howe
Class 11.	Mrs M.B. Lamb

By 1954, the school had over 500 children on the roll (180 more than it was originally designed for) and a report by HM school inspectors indicated that the premises were scarcely adequate.

Despite being well furnished and equipped, space limitations meant that one of the twelve classes was being taught in unsatisfactory conditions in the school dining room. Use of the Assembly Hall for Music, Drama and PE had to be curtailed due to the high level of pupils, which was to the detriment of the subjects for which the school had already earned a high reputation.

MONKSEATON WEST COUNTY PRIMARY SCHOOL

OFFICIAL OPENING

May 11th, 1949

PROGRAMME

1. Hymn *Praise My Soul*　　　　H. F. Lyte. Tune Goss

2. Chairman's Remarks
   　　　　Ald. F. B. Hindmarsh, J.P.

3. Song *When Daisies Pied.*　　　Shakespeare. Music Dr. Arne
   　School Choir

4. Song *O Lovely May.*　　　　Gauntlett. Music Mozart
   　School Choir

5. 　　　　Professor Brian Stanley
   Director of the Institute of Education, Durham University.
   　　　supported by
   　County Councillor Rev. R. E. Robson

6. Song *Begone Dull Care.*　　　17th Century. Music Brahms
   　School Choir

7. Vote of Thanks
   　H. M. Spink, Esq., M.C., M.A., B.Sc., Director of Education.

The Official Opening Programme, 1949.

In spite of these handicaps, along with staffing difficulties, the school continued to provide outstanding education for boys and girls aged between seven and eleven.

The school flourished over the years and in June 1964, the headmaster, Mr Albert Ford died after serving for 15 years from its opening. A school shield was later bought and dedicated to his memory.

The shield was awarded to the winners of competitions between the four school 'House Teams', taking into account academic, sporting merit and class behaviour. Following changes to the education system in recent years, the school was renamed Appletree Gardens First School to cater for the needs of children up to 9 years of age.

The brand new Monkseaton West County Primary School, Appletree Gardens in 1949.

VALLEY GARDENS SECONDARY MODERN SCHOOL

In April 1954, the Urban District of Whitley Bay received its charter of incorporation as a Borough and, at the same time, the foundation stone of the first new Secondary School to be built within its boundaries since the war was laid, and soon the school which became better known simply as 'Valley Gardens' began to take physical shape.

The two events were not directly related, but each had its origin in the same factor; the steady growth in size and importance of Whitley Bay as a flourishing community and a steady increase in population. Because of this growth, the responsibilities of the Education Committee to provide facilities for education also increased in order to comply with the requirements of the Education Act of 1944.

In all other areas of the county, the Education Committee's first priority was the provision of Primary schools for infants and juniors. From thereon, Monkseaton West Junior School and Langley Avenue Infant and Junior Schools were built catering for up to 3,000 pupils under the age of eleven. It then remained to provide for these children when, after reaching the age of eleven, they would pass into the Secondary Schools.

A swollen child population had already caused severe overcrowding in the two existing Secondary Modern Schools, and this was dramatically eased when building work was complete and Valley Gardens School opened its doors to the first intake of pupils in September 1956.

The main portion of the school building was in two storeys and designed to accommodate 450 boys and girls, consisting of an Assembly Hall, a smaller Hall, Eight Classrooms, three Housecraft Rooms, two Science Laboratories, one Art Room, one Craft Room, Woodwork and Metalwork Rooms, a Gymnasium, Dining Recess, Kitchen and a Library. Cloakrooms and Locker Rooms were provided on the ground floor. The school was surrounded by excellent playing field facilities.

The total cost which was inclusive of site, buildings, furniture, equipment and the laying out of the grounds was £161,868. Designed by Mr. C.C. Brown, the County Architect, construction work was carried out by Messrs. Hastie D. Burton of North

Shields. The school was officially opened at 2.30pm on Tuesday 9th July 1957, by Mr. G.R. Hanson BA, the Registrar of Kings College, Newcastle.

Prior to school reorganisation in the 1970s, the building changed status from that of a Secondary Modern to became known as Valley Gardens Middle School. The school motto is: 'What do you want to achieve'.

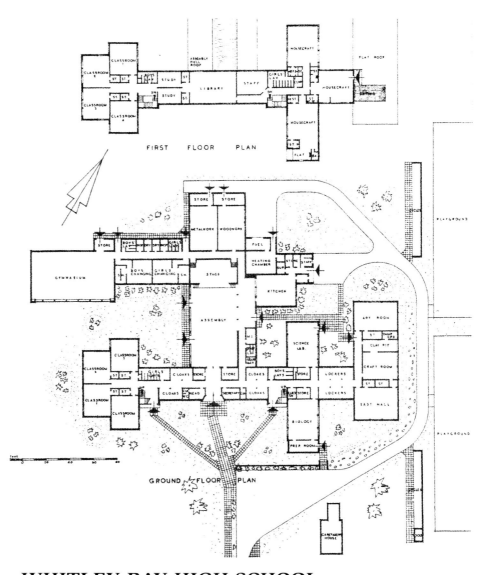

FIRST FLOOR PLAN

GROUND FLOOR PLAN

Right: A 1954 plan of Valley Gardens School.

WHITLEY BAY HIGH SCHOOL

Despite what the name suggests, Whitley Bay High School is situated close to the heart of Monkseaton Village and is really a part of the more modern history of the area. Originally opened and built as Whitley Bay County Grammar School, the main buildings are located near to the end of the present Deneholm, just to the east of the track which led towards Monkseaton Red House Farm.

Typically the school is of a modern pre-fabricated construction style, lacking in aesthetics and elegance but practical for its purpose. Designed by County Architect; Mr C.C. Brown, the main contractor was Gilbert Ash Ltd. Building work commenced on 30th March 1961. Capable of accommodating up to 1,080 boys and girls, the first pupils were admitted on 10th September 1962 with the official opening taking place some fifteen months later on 6th December 1963 by the then Minister of Education; Rt. Hon. Sir Edward Boyle M.P. Building costs, including furniture and fittings totaled £546,000, (compared to the £161,868 cost of the nearby Valley Gardens Secondary School which had been built just six years earlier).

After reorganisation in 1974, it became better known as Whitley Bay High School. During much of the schools lifetime, there has been a regular programme of renovation work, resulting in many alterations and extensions to the original structure which has enabled it to grow considerably in size.

The school is now a mixed Comprehensive School catering for age groups between 13 to 18 years and for a number of years has been heavily oversubscribed. For example in January 2008 the roll of pupils was 1,596, of which 535 occupied places in the Sixth Form. At this time, there were 167 members of staff (108 teaching and 59 support staff).

PEOPLE AND ORGANISATIONS

BOBBY THOMPSON

Robert Michael Thompson (Bobby Thompson) was an icon and perhaps one of the most legendary comedians the North East of England has ever known. Born on 18th November 1911 at Penshaw, Co. Durham he was the youngest of seven children. His life is a story on its own, and a lot of further reading is available in a book by Dave Nicolson entitled: *Bobby Thompson – A Private Audience*.

Bobby Thompson was quite a private man, however he was also a man who had the ability to make people laugh, and for most of the time his image was usually projected on the stages of many of the local clubs and theatres as an emaciated figure, wearing a sloppy threadbare jumper (or 'Gansey'), worn out plus-fours, slippers, a flat cap and a smouldering 'Woodbine' tab. His stage character perhaps embraced that of 'Andy Capp'.

Early in his career, Bobby played a harmonica in the Billy Bankhead Harmonica Band in Washington, and it was Billy who nicknamed him as 'The Little Waster', and the name simply stuck with Bobby during his lifetime.

Bobby performed in many venues throughout the North East, and the central theme of his act was that of debt and pretension with only three or four variations to it; however he endeared audiences with his own brand of North East humour wherever he performed.

Bobby came to live in Monkseaton in 1961 after responding to a press advertisement for rented accommodation at No. 20 Princes Gardens. The house was soon secured, and Bobby lived there for 27 years with his wife Phyllis and later with his housekeeper Cissie.

One of his quips on stage was; *"Of course, I live in Munkseet'n – in a detached hoose. Its faalin' away from the rest"*.

Bobby soon became an established face in the village, and for many years was a regular at all three pubs in Monkseaton, but his preferred option was always the Black Horse.

Bobby Thompson on stage at the Pheasant Pub, North Shields in 1973 – dressed in the way he was best known to millions.

In the 1960s, the winter season saw a coal fire burning in the bar of the Black Horse and Bobby would often materialise through one door to warm his hands and his backside for a few minutes before disappearing out the opposite door on his way to the 'bookies' or the local shops. Occasionally Bobby would sit down and enjoy a bottle of brown ale or two (sometimes 'ticking it on the slate'), and many are the times when he would engage himself in a game of dominoes and entertain his friends in the pub with his wit and humour. On one occasion, Bobby was actually barred from the Black Horse for alleged cheating at dominoes, but he was a very good player where the memory was all important. One of his best domino partners was a certain Doctor from Marine Avenue who had an arrangement with Bobby where he would write out a sick note in the bar for his son, Michael so that he could take time off school to accompany Bobby to Redcar and York race meetings!

Princes Gardens, Monkseaton.

Bobby was a non-practicing Catholic, and another visitor to the Black Horse was Father Cass, who was also a great friend of the Thompson family. The banter between them was always funny.

Bobby loved living in Monkseaton and he loved the people he met there. He was a local personality, but as far as Bobby was concerned, he was just another resident, and was accepted for that reason alone. It had nothing to do with his fame as a comedian on stage.

Bobby had always been a gambling man, and this was certainly a weakness of his. He was happy to walk down to Alan and Paddy Dawson's bookies shop on Front Street, and spend the afternoon there as just another punter. He had a great friend in Alec Lewis, a wealthy gambler who also lived in Monkseaton and the pair of them would regularly bet together at both Dawson's and Ladbrokes in Whitley Bay. Many hours were spent at the Monkseaton bookmaker's shop which in those days was run by William Dawson, who also had the nearby barber's shop where Bobby would also go for a haircut.

William Dawson's barber's shop stood on the corner of Front Street and Coronation Crescent.

Notable visitors to Bobby's house in Princes Gardens included Danny la Rue who came on two occasions to see who he described as 'The U.K's most under rated comic'. Ken Dodd who was in awe of Bobby was invited along for afternoon tea whilst appearing at the Whitley Bay Playhouse and David Jason also called one morning for a bacon sandwich whilst appearing in pantomime with Bobby at the Theatre Royal, Newcastle. David had not previously been able to understand why Bobby got such an ovation before he even spoke a word, but he soon learned! Perhaps the biggest visitor of all to Bobby's house was Mohammed Ali, the championship boxer who arrived completely unannounced with a man called Jimmy Stanley, a local scrap man from Newcastle who had organised his North East visit. Later, Bobby was presented with a signed photo/portrait of Ali with a personal message to the 'Little Waster' which he treasured.

The widely known Noble organisation opened a pub on Wallsend High Street during the 1970s which they named The Little Waster, as a tribute to Bobby Thompson. After operating for several years, the pub closed and so they presented Bobby with a life size Little Waster model which had stood as his representation in the pub during its existence.

Bobby was honoured, and kept this model in a cupboard at the top of the stairs in Princes Gardens, and there is a story that during an attempted burglary at the house, the intruders opened the cupboard only to see what they thought was Bobby standing there, so they fled from the property empty-handed. The story was covered by the local papers soon afterwards.

Bobby died on 16th April 1988 at Preston Hospital, North Shields aged 76 years. His funeral took place at his birthplace in Penshaw, Co. Durham however after the cremation; Bobby's family brought his ashes back to the area and arranged a private ceremony conducted by Father Cass at Whitley Bay Cemetery. His remains were buried in his wife, Phyliss' grave but her headstone does not show his name.

Bobby Thompson was well loved and well respected by everyone in the North East. His memory lives on and he will be fondly remembered for many years to come.

Bobby Thompson – The Little Waster.

Off stage, Bobby, checks out the odds in Dawson's bookmaker's shop, Monkseaton, c.1970.

ROBERT DAVIDSON

Robert Davidson was a prominent figure in the Old Village of Monkseaton. He was born at Lily Cottage on Front Street, Monkseaton on 5th June 1837 and for a time worked for his father, George Davidson who ran the Village Blacksmith, Cartwright and Joiners shop which was situated on Percy Terrace, next to the Black Horse. In 1871, Robert took over the business and employed four apprentices. After his marriage, Robert moved into Rose Cottage on Chapel Lane (formerly the Three Horse Shoes Inn), and played a significant part in village life, as in addition to his original trade, he opened up a part of Rose Cottage as a grocery shop where he also ran an insurance book. He was also the overseer and collector of poor rates for Monkseaton and Preston Townships and also the registrar for births and deaths for the Whitley sub-district.

On 7th September 1904, the Blacksmith and Cartwright's shop were put up for auction, and became Scott and Robson's grocery store.

Robert Davidson died on 15th September 1919 and was buried in St Paul's Churchyard at Whitley.

The letter reproduced below was written by Robert Davidson and dated 21st December 1907. Written in the style of the day, the letter gives his account of Monkseaton along with some personal memories and recollections of his boyhood in the village some sixty years earlier, taking us back to around 1847.

MONKSEATON
December 21st 1907

Dear Sir,
Knowing as I do, the interest you take in anything connected with my Native Village and the zeal you have always shown in whatever pertains to its welfare, I have been vain enough to hope that some of the memories of my boyhood might be interesting to you. The general aspect of the village some 60 odd years ago was quite different to what it is today. The Front Gardens, enclosures and trees, which add so much to its present beauty, were at that time almost entirely absent. I said 'Village' Sir, but in the somewhat vulgar vernacular of the period (juvenile especially), it was 'The Toon'. Westward was 'up the Toon' and Eastward was 'doon the Toon', and the intervening space between the opposite door steps was the 'Toon Gyet' or Town Gate.

Read this as you would Gallowgate or Pipewellgate, being simply a way or road, thus the divergent road leading to what was practically a little suburb was a Byegate, hence the name, but this last is merely a hypothesis of my own. Up the middle was the cart road with an open channel by the side, as there were no recognised footpaths. Once a week the good housewives 'Swept the Doors', and the space so swept was used by pedestrians in going 'up and doon the toon'. Between this and the cart road opposite the farm buildings, were the Byre Middens. The vacant places not so occupied were used for games, Quoits being a favourite with the men, the young pitmen often playing at marbles.

A distinguishing feature was the 'Big Stone', a large whin boulder located at the junction of what is now Chapel Lane and the Main Street, the place being now occupied by a street lamp (within a few yards). The Lighting and Watching Act had not then been passed. Any outside operations requiring more light than that reflected by the cottage windows was obtained by using lanterns of punctured tin, the illuminant being the homely, but now despised tallow dip. As for the Watching, the sole Guardian of the Peace was old Andrew Todd, who likewise kept the highways of the township in order. Neither were there any of the beneficient influences of the Public Health Act in operation. The only system of drainage being kundy-open channel and ditch, the last named, black as the fabled styx, winding its cosy, slimy way down what is now Marine Avenue towards the sea.

You will see on referring to extracts from the Minute Book, that your own dear father was in the forefront of that early struggle for Sanitary reform, which has culminated in the improved conditions of life which we enjoy today.

The Big Stone and the Black Horse corner were the recognised goals for our juvenile games, such as Witty, Witty Way and 'Shinny' – a rude type of the modern Hockey, played with almost as much ferocity as present day Football. The weapons were such like cudgels as could be had, an old walking stick being considered the 'acme of equipment'. 'Shin your sides' was the warning cry, and its observance was duly enforced on the shins of the offender 'out of line'. The ball was generally an old cork bung from the brewery.

Monkseaton Village, from a painting by John Falconar Slater.

A record goal, made through the Black Horse window, however, caused a temporary lull in this form of recreation, and severely tested the skill of the landlord (Mr Henry Whitfield) as an amateur detective. The Black Horse gable end, minus the present doorway, was the 'Bay' for games at Ball, the 'boorie' for marbles being made anywhere. But, Dear Sir, despite the primitive character of the means of enjoyment, which we, as children had, there was at least room to play our games – a privilege which the improvements in the village in some measure, at least, seems to have deprived the present generation. I think, that where children live in any appreciable number, a free playground ought to be provided for their use. Adults, as a rule, are able to provide these things for themselves.

The means of education in the village were meagre indeed. Old Clark in Byegate, and Macdonald in the corner of the Fold, and subsequently an old army pensioner in the Wesleyan Chapel. It is doubtful whether the curriculum in any of the above cases would have been satisfactory to Mr Birrell (President of the Board of Education) or the House of Lords.

There was quite a troup of lads and lasses went to Cullercoats, to a school kept by Mr William Moffatt and his sister. It was held in the Congregational Chapel there, or as the fisher fold termed it 'Jacks Cheppel', the Rev. Archibald Jack from North Shields conducting service in the building on Sundays. Its weekday name was 'Billy Moffat's Skyull'. Mr Moffatt was a kind man and a competent teacher, and despite his leather belt, enjoyed the affection and unbounded confidence of his pupils. It never came into our heads for a moment to dream that there was anything 'beyond his ken'. Forgive me if I quote; *"The more we gazed the more the wonder grew, that one small head could carry all he knew"*.

The farmers' sons were sent to finish at Leitche's (Old Waller's) in Albion Road, North Shields. It was like going to college, and they looked down upon us poor little disciples of Moffatt.

There were no daily papers with their lst, 2nd, 3rd and special editions. Mr Henry Dunn of the Village Farm, and my father, shared a weekly – the *Newcastle Courant*. The paper was divided and the halves exchanged in the middle of the week, and even after my marriage, I sometimes paid a penny for the 'loan' of the said weekly, now defunct. The occupiers of the various farms were: East Farm, Mrs Nixon; West Farm, I cannot remember; North West Farm, Mr Henry Davison; South West Farm, Mr John Nicholson; North Farm, Mr Joseph Dunn, succeeding Mr Henry Whitfield; ByeGate Farm, Mr Joseph Dunn, succeeding some maiden ladies named Chater; Red House Farm, Mr Moor; Burnt House Farm, my maternal grandfather, George Ramsey; Seaton Ville Farm, Mr Fenwick Aynsley; Rake House Farm, Mr Joseph Fenwick; The Village Farm, Mr Henry Dunn. The Village Farm steading was rebuilt a little over 50 years ago. I remember the old Farm House with its spacious, stone-flagged kitchen in front, with a passage leading to the back kitchen in between. Next, westwards, were the byres, turnip house etc., and at the West End, next to South West Farm, was a stable in the street, and a passage leading into a cottage looking into the farmyard. This was occupied by Betty Pigg and her daughter, the village dressmaker (Village Room site) – who married Mr Richard Yellowley, brother to Mrs Dunn. Mr Yellowley died at Earsdon, at an advanced age only a few weeks ago.

A painting of Monkseaton Brewery as it was in 1877. (Artist unknown)

There were no fleet-footed steeds, with ornate equipages, for the delivery of milk in those days, the lacteal fluid being conveyed to North Shields on the back of the patient ass. I can well remember Doctor and Jenny, who alternately carried out this duty on the Village Farm. A barrel was slung at each side, and a boy sat astride between.

The barrels were closed with a cork bung, and the very frequent absence of this necessary article when required, owing to the negligence of the 'Boy' earned for him the nickname of Bungey – a commonly accepted term in use at the present day. Shortly after this, carts were provided for the donkeys and, afterwards ponies began to come into general use. The farmer had a dispensing agent in the town called a 'Milk-Wife'. And now Sir, if you could, in imagination, go back to that remote period of time when I was a boy, and we foregathered, say on a Saturday, at the 'Brewery End' (a local term), We might have a 'dander roond the toon', taking note of a few characters as we pass along.

First a 'keek' at the 'Brewery'. A dray cart is being loaded with ale at the loading hole, – a sort of dock formed so that the barrels could be run straight off the ground into the cart. One or two pigs are investigating a heap of exhausted hops thrown from the cooler windows. The ale is cooling on the floors above. The farmers' carts are standing about, waiting their turns at the grain spouts, which projected outside. Old Tommy Lowery, the Brewer, is giving the driver of the full cart his 'Horn' of ale before leaving. The ale, after cooling, was tunn'd into barrels on gauntries standing in rows on the cellar floors. The fermentation took place in the barrels, the yeast overflowing out of the bung holes into the gauntries, was gathered into a large tub standing just inside the main building, and after being sufficiently diluted with water and whisked around with a heather besom, the dipper was hung over the edge, and it was ready for sale. The article 'Made in Germany' had not then arrived. Up in the higher regions, the process of malt making was carried on.

We might now slip through and look at the new stable, with malt floors above. The old stable was burnt down about 65 years ago, 5 horses perishing in the flames. Their bodies were, I believe buried in Chamberlain's Meadow, then in the occupation of Mr William Davison, who owned the brewery. 'Old Spanker' alone was induced to leave, and that with difficulty, by a door opening into the yard of Monkseaton House. A subsequent fire a little over 50 years ago, at which I was present assisting, destroyed that part of the building in which the machinery was situated.

What is now the Monkseaton Arms was the Brewery Office. There were somewhere between 30 and 40 houses in the neighbourhood, some at South Shields tied to the Brewery. The legend of 'Monkseaton Entire' which they displayed, was considered to be the 'sine qua non' of excellence in the beverages supplied.

Old 'Barney Nail', or as he described himself in some verses which he wrote, the man they call Bernard O'Neil, who 'buys all his baccy, but steals all his ale', one of the old-timers connected with the Brewery, is sweeping in front of Monkseaton House and anathemising the pigs, who at that time enjoyed the freedom of the streets. A little Irishman – he was an ever ready and persistent defender of the dogmas of the Roman Catholic Faith, and often in passing my father's shop

Coronation Row.

on his way home would fling down his 'Gage of Battle', and many a doctrinal contest was the result. But Dear Sir, on calm reflection how poor and insignificant do earth's distinctions of class and creed appear in the light of that all embracing love which is divine. A love which reaches to the lowest and covers their utmost need, and we may well believe, that as the ages roll on in the great heart of the eternal, will ever be the remembrance that God made man in His own image, and that existing in 'every' human life are the potentialities of an immortal soul.

Past the Chapel of Ease (now 'The Cottage'), Coronation Row extended to the Black Horse – doors and shutters painted black, door frames and sashes painted white, outside walls white-washed, floors of brick or flags, some of them a mixture of lime and small coals. This was the general type of cottage scattered over the village, the majority of which have now given place to better dwellings. In one of the cottages lived old Jack Smith and Nanny his wife. The old man in his younger days, worked in the Ironstone pit on The Links. He was very popular with the farmers as a 'First Footer', his favourite toast being "May the wing of Friendship never lose a feather".

In the middle of the Row lived Miss Smith, who, owing to her avowed

Percy Terrace, from a painting by Clement Nixon.

attachment for the feline race, was called 'Cat Sally'. Her little shop with its bow window was an attraction, especially with a small coin getting warm in the pocket. A Farthing was not a despised coin in those days and the little boy who was sure of one every Saturday morning was looked up to as a person having an allowance. Its purchasing power in this instance is two Black Bullets, (one a piece) no diminutive, multiflavoured, factory made articles these Sir, but the real home made substantial satisfying sweetness evolved from Golden Syrup and Sugar.

And now round the Black Horse corner we come to my father's Blacksmith Shop, (the site now occupied by Mr C. Scott's Shop). Down a little back street, behind Coronation Row, we pass Barney's Cottage and come to a Cartwright and Joiners Shop and Stable at the very bottom. Mr John Duxfield and his partner Mr James Davison occupied the premises after the death of Mr J. Davidson, who had won the respect of all who knew him, and Mr Duxfield wishing to retire, my Father bought his business and stock, and it was here that I served my time. Through the shop at the North side was a large yard with a gateway opposite to East Farm. The Saw Pit of somewhat fatiguing memory and a Jargonelle Pear Tree reaching over the wall into the Garden of Monkseaton House, was in the North East corner (the site is now occupied by No 1

Percy Terrace), west of the yard and up to the Blacksmith's Shop was Garden. The path in front of Percy Terrace is laid on the old wall.

The Ship Inn, occupied by Captain Duxfield, was a favourite place of call for Sailors travelling between the Ports of Shields and Blyth. In the Stack Yard of North West Farm there used to be a Cottage, and here lived the Village Piper, James Maddison with his sons who were

The Fold, c.1910.

hired as hands with Mr Henry Davison. The old man having lived past the age for permanent employment and having part leisure was also the proud possessor of a pair of Highland Bagpipes, which he was fond of playing in season and out of season, his favourite tune being 'Johnny Cope', and should any wandering Highland minstrel chance upon the scene, Old Jimmy made a point of playing him off the ground.

One of his sons, however, being wearied at night, and after vainly protesting against the din in the home, drew his knife and thrust it into the bag, and with the dying sob of his outraged bellows, poor old Jimmy's musical career was ended.

Immediately to the West was an old farm steading with an open space in front, the only approach to anything like a Village Green. This at a later date was known as the 'Cuddys Field'. The old 'Smiddy', Byre, Stable and Yard, the property of Mr William Brown, Blacksmith (retired), stood on the site now occupied by Murie House and Jessamine House. Mr Brown also partly owned and partly rented the land known as Dickie's Holm.

As we saunter along the 'Fad' first door on the right, we may see old Jack Allan and some of his sons making besoms with heather gathered from the Northern moors. The old man had his pony and cart for hawking them, and as this was the chief sanitary weapon used in the neighbourhood, he did a very good trade.

In the meantime, old Jenny, said to be the mother of nineteen, the major part of whom were scattered, some at Yetholm and other places in the 'North Countree' – used to leisurely go round with her basket of earthernware, supplying any need of that kind, having a pipe and a gossip here and there as she went on. Further on was the Skinnery, with its lime pits and other appliances, where Daniel Miller and Wattie Patterson cured skins for Mr Joseph Dunn, Butcher, of North Farm. The butcher's shop is now a stable in Mr Dryden's yard. The stream which divided the Townships of Monkseaton and

Earsdon was dammed just within the entrance to Dickie's Holm to form a washing place for the skins. Mr Dunn paid Mr Brown £5 per annum for the privilege.

Still in the Fold we come to the Village Mangle, kept by Mrs Graham, whose husband was a lime-burner in the quarry at Hill Heads. They also kept two cows and a donkey, which were herded in the long pastures'. The adjacent lanes having a much larger margin of green than they have at present, the other cottages were principally occupied by artificers in tin and others of the lighter crafts, such as repairing defects in umbrellas, coopering etc.

In leaving the Fold, we pass the cottage occupied by George (Geordy the Jockey). He worked for some time in the brewery and likewise broke in young horses for the farmers and others, a somewhat dangerous calling. It was said, and we youngsters quite believed that his skull had been repaired with silver plates. Peggy Quarry crippled with rheumatism, and her son Willie lived here also. Willie had a horse and cart, leading coals and hawking yeast and small beer.

Across the street, just a peep through the end door at Mr Dunn's yard and butcher's shop, after perhaps a hasty exit past the Big Stone, we come to Peggy Lowery's or the Three Horse Shoes, a little wayside pub, now the receipt of custom for Poor Rate. This, with the cottage adjoining, was partly rebuilt by my father 45 years ago, who brought his business from the opposite side of the street and lived here for a short time before removing to Preston.

Past the Wesleyan Chapel, some particulars anent which you already have, we come to – may I call it Fort Ramsey with its wooden artillery, trained on Shields Lonning? Mr Robert Ramsey and his wife Bella lived here. Robert was a 'Datal man', doing hedging or whatever agricultural work he could obtain, also cultivated his

Bygate Road, from a painting by Clement Nixon.

garden, which 'Failing the acquisition of Naboth's vineyard', was sufficiently replete with herbs to have excited the cupidity of King Ahab. As to the 'Yarbs', Bella had the reputation of knowing what they were severally 'Gud for' in this and some other matters being necessary to the well being of the community.

Down the Lane past Stack Yard and Gardens the next dwelling house was Rock Cottage. One of the inmates was Martha Young who went round the collieries and neighbourhood with her Yard Stick and Pack. In behind, lived Robert Duxfield (Bob Dyuk) the Village Carrier and had his stable there. After his death William Ackinclose or (Willie Akkum), a pit sinker who married his daughter carried on the business.

In Byegate some 8 or 9 families lived, Old Clark and his School (the Old Wesleyan Chapel) being at the east end. In the middle was a brick oven large enough to bake sufficient bread for the lot in one batch. There was a similar oven at Hill Heads and another at Fiddler's Green or Marden.

In coming back to the Main Street we leave the Fancy Field. Now built over on the right in this field was the 'Fancy Well', now covered over by the Railway, this was one of the water supplies. Nixon's well on the East Farm, now filled up was another, and the 'Far Well' on the same farm some distance North but this was only used when other supplies failed. The chief supply and the one mostly used was from a drain made kundy fashion with flags which tapped the gravelly subsoil near the top of Cauldwell Lane. Its course was down the Village, past the front of Percy Terrace to an opening still to be seen. The water could be diverted into the reservoirs in the garden of Monkseaton House, or left to flow into Nixon's pond, the usual watering place for horses and cattle.

The exit was called the low drain and the opening opposite Bromley Place was the middle drain, and another opening further up west was the high drain, but there were times when these supplies were woefully insufficient.

The Cottages opposite the Brewery up to Miller's shop, now Clayton House, were chiefly occupied by men working at Whitley Pit. Mr Robert Miller, who was a substantial Provision Merchant and Ship owner, built a shop and block of property in Sidney Street and Lovaine Place, North Shields, and subsequently went there to live. Next to this, in Gourd Cottage, lived Dr Brown, who kept a saddle horse, his practice being chiefly outside the village. Next door to this, in what is called Lily Cottage, my father lived, and it was here that I made my first appearance on this mundane sphere on the 5th day of June 1837.

In the next house lived the village shoemaker, and in the yard behind lived old Captain Dunn, also a man, who on account of his shifting, visionary, hither and thither schemes for making money, was called 'Puff and Dart'. I forget his real name. He occupied the large garden reaching through to the back lane. It is one of my earliest recollections being allowed, with some 4 or 5 others, to follow him into his garden, and being allowed to 'weed the beds'. This privilege we enjoyed very much, but alas, in the case of myself and another, who failed to differentiate between a blade of grass and, I think it was called a 'Scallion' in its early youth, we were driven from his Eden, and the door was shut. How these early memories cling. The sense of his unkindness remains with me today.

The next house was occupied by Mr W. Brown the retired Blacksmith. Mr Brown was a devout Churchman, and used to ring the bell for service over the way. And now we are back to the Village Farm, with all its up to date improvements. It's Church Militant, and a long felt want supplied in the Village Room, which, with its complete equipment for the full enjoyment of the various means of Social and Educational advancement, may not inaptly be termed the 'Heart of the Village Life'.

And now, Sir, in conclusion in looking back over the three score and ten years of my own life in the Old Village, there are many things that I would fain I had left undone and many opportunities for good neglected, yet I am thankful for friendships that are dear to me and the memory of other's equally dear that are past, and most of all, for this, that I am permitted in the eventide to shelter beneath the mercy of a pardoning God, and cherish a hope that one day in his own good time, when called to cross over to the other side, I may in the brightness of our fathers homeland, meet with those who have shared in the joys and sorrows of earth.

I am Dear Sir,
Yours Faithfully,
Robert Davidson

Front Street, c.1902.

WILLIAM WEAVER TOMLINSON

An accountant by profession, William Weaver Tomlinson was a prominent local historian and writer and his residence for many years was 1 Victoria Villas, Whitley Bay. Early Wards Directories show that by 1911/12 he was living in Hawthorn Gardens, Monkseaton at a house called 'Lillevilla'. The name of Tomlinson is well known by all those having an interest in the local history and topography of Northumberland, particularly during the latter part of the 1800s and early 1900s. Amongst his various writings, he compiled perhaps the most informative book ever written about the county; *Tomlinson's Comprehensive Guide to Northumberland*, which was first published in 1888 and is still used to this day as a basis for much local history research. Another significant publication was called *Historical Notes on Cullercoats, Whitley and Monkseaton* which first appeared in 1893. This book takes the reader on a fascinating journey through Cullercoats, Whitley, Monkseaton and Tynemouth as the writer describes all the interesting streets, buildings and history associated with these places in the late 1800s. The book also formed a foundation on which to compile this publication. Tomlinson died on 26th November 1916 at Monkseaton.

The following two extracts relating to Monkseaton Village were written around the turn of the 1900s by William Weaver Tomlinson the first of which is entitled:

VILLAGE ROOMS IN OLD MONKSEATON

In an old advertisement relating to Whitley House (*Newcastle Courant* dated 27th April 1817), it is stated: 'A pew in Tynemouth Church is attached to the house, from which it is only two miles distant'. Only two miles! yet they sufficed to keep many of the good folk of Monkseaton at home on a Sunday. In these circumstances the Vicar of Tynemouth (the Rev. Christopher Reed) decided to hold services in the village, and a fund was started for the purpose of providing a. room. The subscribers, many of them 'old standards' in the place were: William Davison (Brewer and Shipowner), Miss Mary Henzell, (Daughter of Peregrine Henzell of the Glasshouses,

Front Street looking east in 1905.

who lived in Belvedere House, Whitley), Thomas Wright (of Whitley Park), several Farmers in the township, namely Henry Dunn, Joseph Nixon, Henry Nicholson, and Fenwick Aynsley, Joseph Dunn (Butcher and Fellmonger), John Duxfield (Innkeeper), besides John Tinley and Joseph Laing jnr. (Solicitors of North Shields).

A room measuring 37 feet long by 17 feet wide and 10 feet in height with accommodation for 140 persons was obtained by throwing two of the cottages adjoining the Black Horse into one. A bell-turret was then added, completing what the directories called 'An Episcopal Chapel of Ease in Monkseaton'. It was opened for Public Worship by the Rev. Christopher Reed on the 28th April 1839.

Subsequently a service was held in it every Sunday afternoon, usually conducted by the Curate, who drove out from North Shields in a cab. The natives of the village for one generation at least, were baptized in this room, one of them being Mr Henry Nicholson of Newsteads.

After the sub-division of the parish of Tynemouth in 1860, a wing of Whitley Hall, then occupied by Mr M.W. Lambert, was fitted up as a temporary church at a cost of £200 and the services were transferred from Monkseaton to Whitley.

Sixty-six years ago, Monkseaton was being paragraphed as a 'spirited little village' on account of the part it was taking in a movement, which the local press described, somewhat grandiloquently as 'The intellectual advancement of the rural population'. The movement was started in the autumn of 1840 by Mr Thomas Harbutt, of the Monkseaton Brewery, and resulted in the formation of the 'Monkseaton, Whitley and Cullercoats Literary Institute'. The object of the institute was to promote the cause of mental improvement in the district by means of a library and reading room, classes for the teaching of reading, writing (cyphering), grammar, etc. and popular lectures on literary and scientific subjects.

The first meeting of the Institute was held on the 26th January 1841, when a lecture was delivered by the Rev. Archibald Jack, an Independent Minister of North Shields, on 'The Advantages of General Knowledge', in the course of which he described the Colours of the Rainbow, the Powers of Condensed Air and the Effects of Gravitation. The lecture lasted nearly two hours, and must have strained somewhat severely, the powers of endurance of a rural audience. On the 22nd of March, the lecturer was the Rev. John Robertson of Low Fell, and his subject 'Electricity' was accompanied by experiments. At the close of the lecture, Miss Chater presented an electrical apparatus to the Institute.

A lecture on 'The Mind' was given on 29th of March, when the phenomena of Dreams, Somnambulism, and Apparitions, etc. came under review.

The classes for instruction in grammar, etc., were conducted by Mr. Henry Johnston, the Master of the Kettlewell School at North Shields, who also lectured on Astronomy.

The Old Black Horse, c.1905.

A social gathering of the members of the Institute, dignified with the name of 'Soiree', was held on the 24th of May, when speeches were delivered by Dr. Pyle of Earsdon and Dr. Owen of North Shields, as well as by Mr. Love of Whitley and Mr. Nixon of Monkseaton. All of these meetings in Monkseaton, some of them attended by about 200 persons, were held in 'John Duxfield's Long Room'.

Although John Duxfield appears as the Landlord of the Ship in 1841, the 'Long Room' was probably that at the top of the Black Horse, which he occupied in 1834 and subsequent years. One reason for coming to this conclusion is that after tea on the 24th of May, a band of music under the leadership of Mr. Paston of North Shields, appropriately played 'What a Getting Upstairs'.

The next desideratum at Monkseaton, was a public school. How the village had fared in the matter of education during the bygone centuries, we cannot tell, with the solitary exception of a reference to 'Mr. St. Claire of Monkseaton – Schoolmaster'. In the Tynemouth Church Registers, under 1709, there is nothing in our local records to show that the birch-rod ever flourished at Monkseaton, but a school of some kind was kept in 1841 by William Clark. In this year a scheme was set on foot to build a large Public School at Monkseaton, and concerts were organised to raise money for the purpose. The first was held on 24th August and the second on 6th September, in the spacious premises attached to the house of Mr Whitfield, Farmer, which the *Gateshead Observer* described as 'The Assembly Rooms in Monkseaton'.

The first concert was attended by 200 or 300 persons, among whom were Mr Mitcalfe of Whitley Hall, Mrs Fryer of Whitley House, Dr. Meggit of North Shields, and Dr. Pyle of Earsdon. The principal attraction at both concerts was the Apollo Philharmonic Band under the leadership of Mr Lamb, late of the Theatres Royal, London, Dublin etc., which performed selections from 'LeNozze de Figaro' (Mozart), and 'Fra Diavolo' (Auber) etc. Glees were sung at both concerts by Messrs. W & T Gordon Askew and Jackson and it is satisfactory to state on the authority of the *Gateshead Observer* that the songs were executed in no mediocre way.

The moving spirit in all these good works was Thomas Harbutt, who also founded the 'Northern Luminary Lodge of the Independent Order of Oddfellows' at Monkseaton. Unfortunately in the Spring of 1842, he removed from Monkseaton to North Shields. Before leaving, a Public Dinner was given in his honour on the 9th March, in the house of Mr John Duxfield, over which Mr John Tinley presided. A silver cream jug, which had been subscribed for by the workmen at Monkseaton Brewery and others, was presented to him on this occasion. Brief life was the portion of the institutions which he founded in the village. The books of the library were afterwards sold, and those still in existence, some in the possession of Mr Robert Davison, are only memorials of the Literary Institute of 1841. The public school was never built. In 1858, there was a day school conducted by Joseph Wilkins, an old army pensioner, in the little Wesleyan Chapel, which Mr Robert Miller had built in 1843. In 1865 there was a national school in Monkseaton, conducted by Miss Maria Day, in the Church of England Room adjoining the Black Horse, which would probably be closed when the school, built by Mrs Abbott was opened at Whitley in 1870.

The second extract is entitled;

ALONG THE TRACK OF THE OLD WAGGONWAYS IN WHITLEY AND MONKSEATON

Towards the close of the seventeenth century a considerable quantity of coal was being raised in Whitley and Monkseaton, part of which was shipped at the little port of Cullercoats, and part burnt in the Cullercoats Salt Pans and in the Limestone Quarries at Marden. A wooden waggonway (*see page 48*) ran from one end of the township of Whitley to the other, joined about halfway in its course by a branch from Monkseaton.

Though 180 years and more have passed since the waggonway was used, it can still be traced for a considerable distance. The footpath running through the fields behind Whitley Lodge, the Convalescent Home and the Whitley Links Farmhouse to Marine Avenue, recently diverted at its southern end, probably marks the course of the main waggonway, which afterwards passed through the grounds of Whitley Park, of Dennis' Close as it was formerly called, to a point near the Primitive Wesleyan Chapel in North Parade. Here it was joined by the branch from Monkseaton which, starting from the Northern boundary of the township, ran through the fields of Village Farm lying North of

Windsor Gardens from the junction with Queens Road.

Holywell Avenue and Queens Road, across the site of Windsor Gardens and Eastbourne Gardens to Marine Avenue near the foot of Hawthorn Gardens, where taking an easterly direction, it cut across a corner of the 'Whitley Nook Field' and the road leading from Marine Avenue to Whitley, and traversing the field in which are situated the Board Schools, then known as the 'Dovecote Close', passed between the site of the present Whitley Park Hotel and the Lodge, across Park Avenue and Oxford Street, to the point of junction beyond.

32 Victoria Avenue, Whitley Bay.

Twenty or thirty years ago it was usual to see, after the Winter ploughing, a black band stretching across the Dovecote Close, indicating the course of the waggonway. Now there are no traces of the waggonway left in the field.

When we get to North Parade, it is an easy matter to follow the course of the waggonway to Cullercoats. Esplanade Place practically marks the line of it.

The opening in Victoria Avenue is a permanent memorial to the waggonway. It was in recognition of a public right of way acquired by the use of the waggonway as a footpath.

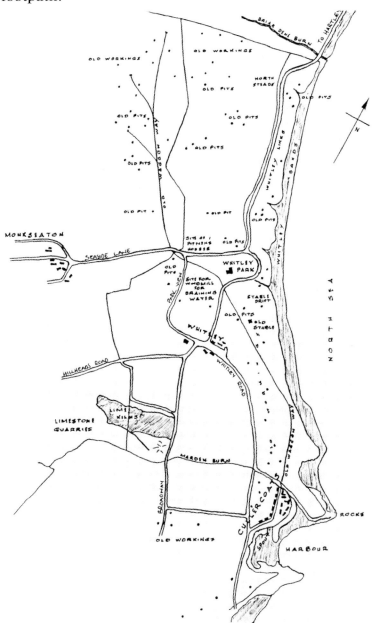

From the gap in Victoria Avenue, the waggonway may be followed by proceeding in a straight line past the end house of Eleanor Avenue to the foot of Cheviot View, and passing behind Rockcliffe and Eastcliffe to the foot of Gordon Square.

From Gordon Square to Grafton Road, it still exists as a footpath, on the west side of the old Rockcliffe Cricket and Football Field.

Through the kindness of Mr T.E. Forster, I am enabled to reproduce a plan of the waggonway *(shown left)* prepared by Mr J.T.W. Bell, probably from the notes of Mr Matthias Dunn, the well known colliery viewer in 1816. It shows very clearly the extent of the colliery workings in Whitley and Monkseaton.

Of the numerous coal pits which are indicated on the plan, only a few can be located at the present day. These are to be found on the Whitley Links, in a small grass field called the 'Clay Bank Close', a little north of Queens Road, at the north east corner of Monkseaton Township, behind Eastbourne Gardens near the builders shed, and in North Parade, about 100 yards from the Promenade.

The rails and sleepers of the main waggonway were of Oak, but on the branches of Birch or Ash. For 8/6 a ten (33 tons and upwards) or 3d a ton, Richard Young of Newcastle, house carpenter agreed in 1704 to maintain the waggonway and branches, and to keep in repair 39 waggons, the terms of the contract being the following:

This sketch by Mr T. Eyre Macklin made in 1893 for Historical Notes on Cullercoats, Whitley and Monkseaton shows the waggonway running from Grafton Road to Cullercoats. Its course may still be followed though with some difficulty, past the end of Margaret Road towards the Whitley and District Laundry, and past the foot of Naters Street and the late Mrs. Nater's old house. The waggonway ran right through old Cullercoats (Brown's Buildings stand on the site of it), to the head of the bank near the present Cullercoats Bay Hotel.

'He shall fix good and sufficient new rails and sleepers of Oak timber, and well and sufficiently ballast the same, and cleanse of stone the gutters and passengers for water on each side thereof in and along the said waggonway, and carry on, make, lay etc. sufficient branches to the main waggonway of Birch, Ash or other sufficient woods and timber, and well ballasted, to the main waggonway from every pit now sunk or hereafter to be so in any of the Monkseaton or Whitley Grounds, and shall lay all the rails on the trunks and staithes, and find good timber for the same, together with the ongates and offgates to and from the same, and keep in repair the main waggonway, branches and rails (Excepting at any time in the year any extraordinary rain or snow shall happen to fall upon the said waggonway and branches, which may occasion unreasonable damage) and leave the wagons in as good a plight as they now are.'

The wagons used in Whitley and Monkseaton were of a comparatively small size, holding 13 bolls, or about 28 cwts each.

They had wheels of unequal size, in order to keep the wagon level on a falling gradient. In three cases where the diameter of the fore wheels was 27 inches, the diameter of the hind wheels was respectively 19, 21 and 23 inches. In another case the diameter of the fore wheels was 31 inches, and that of the hind wheels 25 inches.

A reference to the plan will show that near the Monkseaton Branch of the waggonway, where it crossed Marine Avenue, stood a row of pitmen's houses, occupying a triangular plot of ground, rather more than half an acre in extent, situated on the Whitley side of the

The eastern section of Marine Avenue, from the junction with Ilfracombe Gardens and Park View.

boundary in the angle formed by Marine Avenue and Ilfracombe Gardens.

A line drawn from Mr Weightman's house to Dr. Horseman's will give the base of the triangle, and lines from these points to the new Wesleyan chapel the other two sides. The place occurs in the Tynemouth Parish Registers as early as 22nd May 1679 as 'Pit Houses, viz. between Whitley and Hartley'. In recording in August 1681, the birth of Mary, daughter of James Kirtley of Whitley Pit Houses, the parish clerk added that she was 'Killed by ye engine viz. The wheeles as they report', one of the tragic incidents so common in a mining district.

The pit houses appear to have been afterwards known as the 'Long Row', and though the houses disappeared, the plot of ground continued to be known by that name until 1885, when it was purchased by Mr T.A. Potts, and incorporated with the adjoining field.

In 1720, Monkseaton Colliery was said to be 'Wholly wrought out' and that part of Whitley Colliery which was still being worked, nearly exhausted. The lesees had attempted a fresh winning at Whitley, but after an expenditure of £1,000 had been obliged to abandon the enterprise on account of heavy feeders. They were prepared to risk further capital in the erection of one of the pumping engines of the Newcomen type, which had just been introduced into the district, if terms could be arranged with the lessor. The concessions asked for were not apparently granted, the pits were laid in and the old waggonway fell into disuse. Coal however was still needed for the burning of lime in the quarries at Marden, and was probably obtained from the pits in the 'Clay Bank Close' and from a pit on the west side of Monkseaton Red House.

Mr Chas Dalton Purvis of Earsdon, in a letter dated 8th May 1805 gives the following particulars about Monkseaton Colliery:

'John Brown of Monkseaton, Blacksmith aged upwards of seventy tells me that he has heard one William Barker, now dead, say that he was a wagon man at the above colliery, that the pit was at the west end of Mr Thomas Wright's farm house in the Township of Monkseaton (Monkseaton Red House), and the waggonway passed from thence through the field belonging to Mr Hudson, lying immediately west of Mr Wrights present residence (Whitley Park) by the foot of Whitley, to Cullercoats where the coals were shipped.'

Brown does not recollect the colliery in a working state as a sea-scale colliery, but he recollects Mr Hudson working it for the quarries. He has heard his father say there was no engine and that the water was drawn by horses, and great numbers were 'destroyed by it'.

A waggonway or coal road ran from the 'Clay Bank Close' near the north end of Queens Road along the fence to Holywell Avenue, across the field west of Holywell

Hollywell Avenue, Monkseaton.

47

Avenue, and the Avenue Branch of the North Eastern Railway towards Turpins Lane. Its course is indicated by the post and rail fence in the field west of the Avenue Branch, and by the footpath running parallel and close to Turpins Lane, past the signal cabin and brewery, the end of the village and the garden of Bygate Farmhouse, along the field dyke to Whitley Hillheads. It would no doubt be joined by a branch from the pit situated on the west side of Monkseaton Red House.

In 1810, a cast iron waggonway was made from the Marden Quarries to the Low Lights at North Shields. A branch was made to it from the new pits sunk in 1817 and 1819 near Whitley Hall, the site of one being at the station end of The Crescent, the site of the other at the opposite end.

Ironstone was also worked about this time in the old pits on Whitley Links, the ore being conveyed by a waggonway running across the site of Whitley Park Terrace, past the Avenue Hotel to North Parade. (The bathing machines of Mr Dunn used to stand upon it during the winter months.)

Up North Parade, across the end of Whitley Main Road and past the end of The Crescent to Marden.

The waggonway from the old pit near the Whitley Railway Station may still be traced as far as the road leading from Whitley to Tynemouth. Of the old Whitley waggonway, which was for long a part of the Blyth and Tyne Railway, there are very unmistakable traces behind Marden House, and in fact all the way southward to North Shields.

Although Tomlinson's description of the wooden waggonway at the beginning of this narrative may be somewhat confusing, its route through Monkseaton may have some bearing on the unusual pattern or layout of the back lanes which for no obvious reason cut through the streets to the east of Holywell Avenue and Queens Road, as indicated by the dark line on the map below.

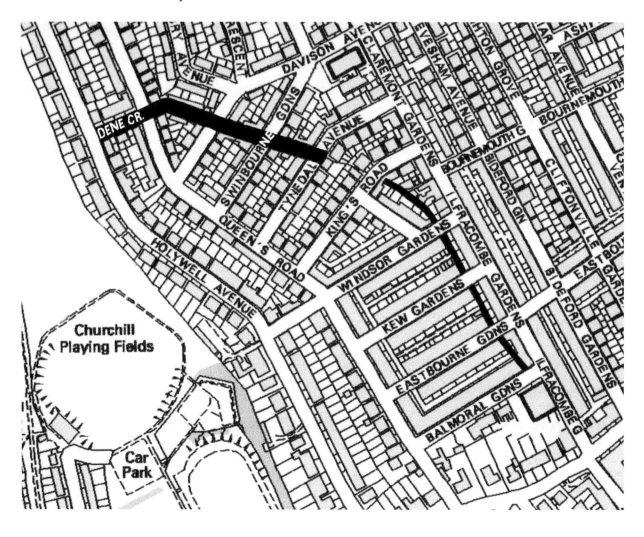

MONKSEATON MORRISMEN

Despite what may be assumed otherwise, the Monkseaton Morrismen and Folk Dance Club (to give it its full title) is really part of the more modern history of the village. Alan and Joyce Brown, assisted by Harry Etherington, founded the club in 1955. During 1949-1950, whilst at King's College, Durham University, Alan came under the influence of Professor W. Fisher-Cassie, a noted authority on the traditional dances of the North East, and the Rapper Sword Dances in particular. Alan and several of his colleagues spent some time collecting and researching material on the various village Rapper traditions, talking to the men who had danced, and remembered the figures and steps.

This group of students became known as the '49ers, and it is thanks to their efforts, that teams are in possession of details of the Rapper Dances, which have been used to supplement the information recorded by Cecil Sharp in the early years of the 20th century. As a result of this work, Alan Brown joined the Newcastle Morrismen on leaving college, but became convinced that there was a need for a team, which would concentrate on the dances of the North East, and be able to perform them publicly to the highest possible standard. In this way, the people of the region would see their traditional dances, and hopefully would keep them alive. During 1955 Alan, Joyce and Harry (an ex-student who had lodged with Alan and Joyce while at King's College) wrote to various dancers they knew, asking if they would like to join the new team. (A copy of that letter was kept, and has pride of place in the first Logbook of the team.)

On commencing his teaching post in 1956 at Whitley Bay Grammar School, (now Marden Bridge Middle School) Alan Brown soon organised a folk dance group and began to run an evening class there. It was that school which became the first meeting place of the Monkseaton Morrismen, which also took advantage of the low hire rates for a classroom! Many of the first members were upper school and sixth formers at the Grammar School, and they were soon performing in public, as Alan had hoped. One of the early shows was at Otterburn Hall, for a group of Hungarian refugees from the 1956 uprising. Joyce remembered it because, as she said, 'They didn't seem to have seen a woman for ages!'

Bryan Jackson was first introduced to country dancing some years earlier when he was a pupil at Appletree Gardens Junior School, and now as a pupil of Whitley Bay Grammar School along with his keen interest in dancing, he went along to Alan Brown's school club. Bryan also played the violin, and of course Alan immediately recognised his talent and potential as a member of the group, and by 1957 Bryan was indeed playing and dancing for the school group, which was his first introduction to the Monkseaton Morrismen, and soon a member he was now taking part in the shows. In the summer of 1958, the Monkseaton Morrismen organised the first Morris Ring Meeting in Whitley Bay, even though the group were not at that time members

The first New Year's day performance outside the Black Horse in 1972.

of the Morris Ring of England, which is recognised as the 'National Association' of Morris dancing clubs. This meeting was held at the Army camp next to St. Mary's Island, as was the second meeting held in 1960. This latter meeting was held in honour of Geordie Osbourne, who had completed 50 years dancing with the Royal Earsdon Sword Dancers, and now as their leader, had received the Gold Badge of the English Folk Dance and Song Society. The Saturday Evening Feast at that meeting was attended by the Deputy Mayor of Whitley Bay, Councillor Cox. He was standing in for the Lady Mayoress, since this was a 'men only' occasion, (being Morris Men!). Councillor Cox was particularly remembered for his larger than life character, and the fact that he had the assembled Morris Men in stitches.

The Monkseaton Morrismen were admitted to the Morris Ring following the first 1958 meeting, and were honoured to be invited in February of 1960 to perform at the showcase Festival of the English Folk Dance and Song Society (EFDSS) at the Royal Albert Hall. This was a major milestone in the history of the team, for this was one of the most prestigious festivals of traditional dance, to which only the best teams in the country were invited. The rehearsals, which were needed, and the blood, sweat and tears which were shed to ensure the team was up to Alan's high standards kept everyone on their toes throughout the winter of 1959 and 1960. The team were to perform the two dances for which they were founded to keep alive, the Northumbrian country-dances, the rants, and the rapper sword dance. At a rehearsal performance in November, at the Alnwick Gathering of the Northumbrian Piper's Society held in the Guest Hall of Alnwick Castle, there was a minor disaster.

The Monkseaton Morrismen outside the Ship, New Year's Day, 2009.

Keith Hanson, the number 1 dancer of the rapper set for the Albert Hall show was not available, so a stand-in was drafted in. As the team completed the dance, and held up the lock of swords, it was noticed too late that a fatal mistake had occurred, and that one of the swords was not properly in place. The lock collapsed and cascaded to the stage floor in front of a major audience! The inquest at the next practice was long and intense, and it goaded the team to work even harder.

In the event, the Albert Hall performances were a major success, and apparently Princess Margaret, who was President of the EFDSS, and present on the Saturday night performance was in fits of laughter as Alan Brown, in his role of Betty, played hide and seek with the follow-spotlights as they tried to keep up with him running around the arena. That particular weekend probably put the Monkseaton Morrismen firmly on the map, with a reputation for the highest standards of dance performance, and as top exponents of the rapper sword dance, a reputation which the team still value very highly, and have striven to maintain over the following years.

After the success of the first Albert Hall performance, the team were soon invited to represent the region at other events. In September 1962 the first foreign tour was organised, and they travelled to Stavanger and Bergen as part of the 'Gateway to Britain' week. This was a tourist and trade event to encourage Norwegians to visit Britain, and several organisations from the North East were involved, including the Whitley Bay Girls' Choir. In 1964 the Monkseaton Morrismen represented the North East at the 400th anniversary of Shakespeare's birth at Stratford. The team were also invited to an international festival in Nuremburg over the Whitsun holiday. This was the 'Sudeten Deutsches Tag', a festival held by the exiled Sudeten Germans. While the event was not particularly memorable, the dancing and visits certainly were. They were billeted with a Breton team, who were pleasantly surprised by these crazy Englishmen, and over several late night parties, including one silent party in a hotel in Bad Kissingen after 10pm. It had to be 'silent' because everyone else had gone to bed, so they danced the rapper in bare feet!

Alan Brown, one of the originators, sadly died in 1983, after collapsing from a heart attack in the street while setting up the first American 'Folkmoot', which was held the following year. Joyce, his wife, died in June 2001, during Monkseaton's Weekend of Dance. This was the first weekend at which she had not been involved in the catering arrangements. Bryan Jackson became one of the longest serving team members, having danced and played for the team since 1957, and for many years was the Squire. Alan Brown's son Peter served as Bagman for 19 years, taking the place of George Mockler who was tragically killed in a car crash just weeks after the death of Alan in 1983. Peter however, stepped down in 2001. He continues to dance, having started in 1967, when he and his brother Roger joined the team for the first time on the tour to Bohemia in what was then Czechoslovakia. His wife Diane, who started dancing in 1968 also remained a committed member of the team. Bryan Jackson's wife Gwyn, who danced for Bedford Fine Companions, made an 'enforced' move north in 1971, and she has danced for Monkseaton ever since! Members of Monkseaton Morrismen have been involved in the national folk dance world. Graham Binless was for many years the North East Field Officer for the English Folk Song and Dance Society, and called dances all around the country. Alan Brown himself was Squire of the Morris Ring of England from 1966 to 1968, and Bryan Jackson was secretary of the Northumberland, Tyne and Wear District of the EFDSS during the late 1970s, to name just three. Peter Brown has an international reputation as one of the foremost teachers of Northumberland/Durham style clog dancing, and has taught this, as well as rapper sword dancing, to groups both at home and in America, at Pinewoods Camp, at the invitation of the Country Dance and Song Society of America. Many other well-known names in the folk world have performed with the team over the years. Kathryn Tickell played and danced with the team in the early 1980s, including the tour in Hong Kong in 1982. This was a memorable experience for all the team, and the members of the band The Occasional Few from Northampton who were also with the team, invited Kathryn and Bryan to join them shortly after to make another record with them. Other well known Northumbrian pipers and singers like Richard Butler, Chris Ormston, Basil and Jean Clough, and Denis Weatherley all at one time or another have joined the team in performances around the North East. Locally based, the Monkseaton Morrismen have performed all over the world, playing and dancing for all types of audiences. It has been a tradition in Monkseaton Village since 1972 that the group perform their traditional dances and Mummers Play outside of the Ship Inn, on New Year's morning, before retiring to the local hostelries for some well earned liquid refreshment! This still remains the highlight of the year for the team, and the audience here in their home village is still one of the largest and most enthusiastic that they perform for.

MONKSEATON MORRISMEN

present

MORRIS & SWORD DANCING

&

MUMMERS' PLAY

at **The Ship & The Black Horse**
12 Noon
NEW YEARS DAY

A 'Mummers Play' is a traditional folk play enacting the ancient ritual of death and resurrection which long predates the Christian version. Usually performed at the Winter Solstice, it represents the death of the old year and the rebirth of the new.

MONKSEATON CRICKET CLUB

For many years, there has been a Cricket Club based in Monkseaton, but very little is known of its origins or early history. Indeed an old Membership and Fixtures card cover indicates its existence as far back as 1908 with some well known local dignitaries listed as Vice Presidents including John Appleby of South West Farm, Reverend G.H.J. Bailey of Monkseaton Methodist Church and Colonel T.W. Elliott of Monkseaton Cottage.

It is probable that the first club was founded sometime during the late 1800s, however the exact site of their playing ground is not known and is simply described on their fixture card as being 'North-west of Monkseaton Old Village' which would possibly suggest it was situated somewhere around the end of Pykerley Lane (Pykerley Road).

In 1908, the playing colours were Chocolate and Yellow and the membership fees per season were 7/6d for players aged over 21 years or 5/- for members under 21 years.

Not to be confused with Whitley Bay Cricket Club, which is situated at West Park, Hillheads, the present Monkseaton Cricket Club was formed in 1969 after an old established club called The Phoenix which was based at Woolsington closed down.

In 1970, the club managed to secure Churchill Playing Fields as a playing venue, and have played there ever since. As a result, the Club was re-named as Monkseaton, joining the 2nd Division of the Tyne & District League. The club badge

MEMBER'S CARD.

Monkseaton Cricket Club.

FIXTURES — Season 1908.

President : Major DOUGLAS.

Vice Presidents.

J. P. Allen, Esq.
Jno. Appleby, Esq.
Rev. G H. J. Baily
Major Brown.
Jos. Charlton, Esq.
W. J. Costelloe, Esq.
Jno. Davison, Esq.
Col T. W. Elliott
Edward Elliott, Esq.
Hy. Fail, Esq.
J. Fenwick, Esq.

J. E. Gibson, Esq.
E. A. Jardine, Esq.
B. McAnulty, Esq.
Hugh Millar, Esq.
Hy. Nicholson. Esq.
W. H. Proctor, Esq.
J. Addison Smith, Esq.
R B. Smith. Esq.
Rev. Ed. Smith.
J. S. Watson, Esq.
J. G. Wood, Esq.

still incorporates the Phoenix as its emblem which was derived from the original club.

The Tyne and District League closed at the end of the 1970 season and Monkseaton were elected to Division 2 of the North East Durham Cricket League. When the club came to Monkseaton, only one member, George Stephenson, was resident in the area but this situation soon changed over the years that followed. The early years were a bit of a struggle on the field of play but as more players were attracted to the club, financial help was available to improve practice facilities and so standards began to improve.

In 1975 the North East Durham League was re-organised enabling Monkseaton to enter a 2nd XI. They celebrated with a resounding win in their first match but that ended their success that season.

In 1976 Monkseaton received the prestigious accolade of Whitley Bay's Club of the Year, a great honour.

In 1978 the Norman Martin Cup was the first silverware to adorn the trophy cabinet since the club joined the N.E. Durham League.

In 1979 Dave Athey, a local policeman, joined the Club and was instrumental in organising a charity match between Monkseaton and a Celebrity XI to raise funds for a local hospital. In front of a huge crowd the likes of TV's Mike Neville and Bill Steel donned their whites in aid of a worthy cause. Further publicity was generated for the club, when Diana Coultrate was selected for the 2nd XI, showing the club's equal opportunities credentials.

David Gibbins joined around this time – a superb batsman in the classical style and he quickly re-wrote the batting records, as well as becoming Chairman in the years to come. His vision of a licensed clubhouse at Churchill Playing Fields failed to materialize, but the 70s ended on a wave of optimism and the next decade was eagerly awaited.

In the 1980s, Monkseaton began to attract good quality young players and this was a golden period for the 1st XI. 1984 saw an amazing 32 matches played during a long hot summer, with 26 victories. The League and Cup double was secured. The Cup Final against Coles Cranes was a nail biting affair as Monkseaton lost 7 wickets in chasing a mere 75 runs but fittingly the skipper Martin Dyer-Smith struck the winning runs.

Having been promoted to Division 1 of the North East Durham League, the 1st XI found the step-up hard and were relegated in 1986, but the arrival of two of the best players to have worn the club's colours provided the catalyst for another golden period. Barry Hills and John Stilborn had both played to a higher standard and came quickly to the fore as 1987's record was: Played 29; Won 21; and with it came a share of the league title. Promotion to Division One did not prove a problem this time as a position in the higher echelons was maintained.

In 1989 Clive Purdy joined the club. He was a top quality spin bowler, hard hitting batsman with a sharp cricket brain and he played a major role in instigating a change of direction for Monkseaton in the next decade as the 1990s proved to be a period of continued development both on and off the field for Monkseaton.

In 1992 they played against some well established sides including their local rivals; Whitley Bay when their team were successful in 9 matches out of 20. Since then, there have been many more success stories behind the club, all of which continue into the present day.

Members of Monkseaton Cricket club in 1984. The photo was taken before a Vaux Cup Semi-Final, and despite losing the game, it was still a very successful time for the club. Back row: George Isley (Scorer), Lawrence Fletcher, Michael Jones, Tony Errington, Andrew Tremble, David Boyd and Jerry Ross. Front row: Ian Graham, Malcolm Birkett, Martin Dyer-Smith (Captain), Bill Heppell and David Gibbins.

WHITLEY BAY FOOTBALL CLUB

Despite the absence of any records, it is believed that there has been a football club in Whitley Bay since about 1890, however there is no indication of where their first playing ground was situated. Originally known as Whitley and Monkseaton Football Club, it was later renamed to Monkseaton FC and in 1950 it became Whitley Bay Athletic after many years in the minor leagues.

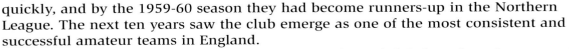

On 14th June 1958 the club was re-formed as a limited company with the name 'Athletic' being dropped from its title. The first Chairman was a Mr J.W.S. Hedworth. The team then simply became 'Whitley Bay Football Club', following which they made a successful application to become members of the Northern League.

The newly named team played their first game at Hillheads Park, their home ground on 27th August 1958 against Durham City, with the result being a goal-less draw. Success came quickly, and by the 1959-60 season they had become runners-up in the Northern League. The next ten years saw the club emerge as one of the most consistent and successful amateur teams in England.

By the mid 1960s a decline in the social side of the club led to plans for a new club house, and within six weeks the project had been completed. The opening ceremony was conducted on 23rd December 1966 by the then chairman of Newcastle United – Lord Westwood. The Seahorse was adopted by the club as its emblem after a competition had been run. The winner was a Mr. Derek Hall who won £1 and a season ticket for his design. The Latin inscription beneath the crest is; 'Ludus est Omnis', which loosely translated means: 'Game is All'.

The first supporters' club was believed to have been established in the Black Horse Inn, Monkseaton in the early 1950s with many subsequent fundraising ventures which included Bingo sessions, social evenings in the Grange Hotel (now the Hunting Lodge), and monthly dances in the Berkeley Tavern at Whitley Bay. This led to the formation of the clubs 'Development Association', which provided revenue from weekly lotteries.

Whitley Bay's team in 1959 was from back left: H. Ross (trainer), Oakley, Newham, Edgar, Walton, Robson, Browell and Charlie Crowe (manager). Front: Stoker, Johnson, Duffy, Bell and Mitten. Charlie Crowe was a former Newcastle United player and was in their FA Cup winning team of 1951.

Whitley Bay F.C. was elected to full membership of the F.A. in 1967 after five years as associates. The Championship came to Whitley Bay in 1966 when, during that year, they reached the Semi-Final of the FA Amateur Cup. Three years later there was another appearance in the Semi-Final, only to be beaten by Sutton United who went on to face North Shields in the Final at Wembley in front of a crowd of 47,000. North Shields beat Sutton 2-1 to win the FA Amateur Cup in 1969.

When floodlights were installed in 1968, a friendly game against Newcastle was the first game played. With the club on the up and up it was decided to apply to the Northern Premier League which proved successful, and since then, they have had several more notable cup runs in recent history.

The team colours are blue and white and their stadium is located adjacent to the Ice Rink, and is capable of holding 4,500 spectators with 250 seats in the main stand. Their success story still continues.

Above: The programme for Whitley Bay's game against local rivals Blyth Spartans in the Northumberland Senior Cup Semi Final in 1992.

Left: Whitley Bay FC team from the 1984-85 season. In the front row, third from the left, is Tony Dawson who made over 300 appearances for the Bay

Below: Action at Hillheads Park.

WHITLEY BAY ICE RINK

Built in 1954, Whitley Bay Ice Rink was the idea of a Mr J. F. J. Smith (best known to many people as 'Icy' Smith) who was the then owner of Durham Ice Rink. A suitable site was secured at the South Eastern edge of West Park, Hillheads, and with a building cost of over £100,000, the rink first opened its doors to the public the following year in May 1955 and has remained under the ownership of the Smith family ever since.

John Frederick James Smith universally known as 'Icy' was born in 1889, at Barnard Castle, County Durham, the thirteenth of fourteen children. Although he first went into the family metal business, he soon decided that the end product was too enduring to encourage many repeat orders and in the pre-refrigerator age, decided to sell the public something that would not last as long – ice.

As his business expanded he moved to Darlington, where he entered public life, and soon became Mayor. He then moved to Durham and bought Bishop's Mill as a place of business. By 1939 this waterside location was to become the site of a new venture – an outdoor ice rink. The rink was initially a spin off from his main business but it became increasingly clear that the development of modern refrigerators would soon put an end to selling large blocks of ice to the public. At the same time Icy's interest in public life continued and he soon became in turn, County Councillor, City Councillor,

'Icy' Smith presenting an award to a young skater at Whitley Bay Ice Rink, c.1955.

Alderman and eventually, Mayor of Durham. During the 1940s the outdoor rink was upgraded, initially with a tent covering and eventually with a more permanent building. As a direct result of the pioneering spirit of this one man, construction of further rinks in the area followed, in Whitley Bay and then the Billingham Forum.

The Whitley Bay Ice Rink was originally designed with a seating capacity of 6,000 persons and the rink now has an actual capacity of 3,600. The area of ice measures 57 metres x 25 metres and it is underpinned by a series of pipes laid on sand through which a refrigerant flows. Layers of ice are built up over the pipes until it reaches the required thickness for skating. This can take days of continuous work. Since its opening there have been very few occasions when the ice has been removed completely, instead it is carefully maintained by specialist staff and equipment, ensuring that the public can use the rink 364 days per year. An ice resurfacing machine runs over the ice between 8 and 10 times per day shaving off a fine layer of surface ice and replacing it with a film of water which quickly freezes to create a suitable surface for skating.

Icy gave his full support to the development of ice hockey in Durham, taking advantage of the skills of Canadian Air Force personnel serving in the area during the war. Ice Hockey in Whitley Bay has a proud history stretching back to 1956 when the first club known as Whitley Bees was founded; however the name was soon changed to the Whitley Braves before eventually becoming better known as the team which exists today as the Whitley Warriors.

The first ice hockey match at the Hillheads rink was played on December 1st 1956. Back then there were no local trained players, so with the rink being owned by the same family that ran the Durham rink, the more established Durham Wasps played games north of the Tyne under the title of Whitley Wasps, In 1964, the Whitley Warriors took to the ice for the first time at Hillheads against a team from the Oxford & Cambridge Universities and Whitley Bay Ice Rink continues to

Whitley Warriors Logo.

56

be the home venue for the Whitley Warriors team.

J.F.J. 'Icy' Smith died in 1965, but he would undoubtedly have been proud to see the number of teams playing ice hockey in Britain today. He would also have been proud of the achievements of 'his' teams, Durham Wasps, Whitley Warriors and the Cleveland Bombers, together with their various junior teams.

In the 1960s part of the building was modified to incorporate a tenpin bowling alley which became known as the 'Ice Bowl'. This area also included pool tables, a snack bar and clubroom; however a decline in demand saw the bowling alley close in 2007. Several more modifications and alterations over the years brought the building up to modern day environmental and safety standards, which included significant soundproofing particularly when the rink became a popular indoor venue for pop

Whitley Bay Ice Rink, 2011

concerts. Between 1982-96 Whitley Bay Ice Rink was the region's foremost concert venue. A list of the performers who have appeared here reads like a Who's Who of the world of entertainment. Kylie Minogue, Sting, Bryan Adams, Wham, Spandau Ballet, Status Quo, Alice Cooper, Chris Rea, Brian May on his first solo tour after Queen, Take That, Oasis and MC Hammer are a few of the international artists who have taken the stage in Whitley Bay.

Many famous skaters, including Torville & Dean at the height of their fame have also visited Whitley Bay Ice Rink and Whitley Bay Ice Skating Club has an active programme for all ages and has regularly produced champion skaters over the years.

RED HOUSE FARM ALLOTMENT SOCIETY

Red House Farm Allotments comprise two separate sections. The beautifully kept main site is situated to the east of Deneholm, between Alder Grove and Churchill Playing fields; however a small triangular extension runs alongside the Metro line between Monkseaton Station and the railway bridge that crosses the line at Relton Terrace.
A majority of the main site which runs adjacent to Alder Grove is located on land which once formed part of Monkseaton Red House Farm on a field which was once referred to as 'Far South Field'. The existing land has never been occupied by buildings and has always been used for agricultural use. Red House Farm Allotment Society was formed during the late 1940s and is self-managed, with a healthy waiting list of people who want to join and share in the pleasures of gardening. A committee is elected each year at the Annual General Meeting which undertakes the day-to-day management of the sites. The society holds many of its shows, events and meetings at Monkseaton Methodist Church, on Front Street, and are always seeking out new members who can give their time either as a Committee Member or as a Volunteer to help with maintaining their sites. In 2009, the society won the prestigious North Tyneside Council Award for the best allotment site in North Tyneside.

The entrance gates to Red House Farm Allotment Site lead off Alder Grove.

CRIME

THE HILLHEADS MURDERS

On the morning of Tuesday 23rd March 1971, the bodies of a local woman and her three children were found in a three bedroomed semi-detached council house, at 37 Priory Avenue, Hillheads. Michael John Small, aged 20 years, lived there with his mother, Elsie Small, and stepfather, Robert Thornton Small, along with his stepsisters, Janet aged 14 years, Jacqueline, aged 8 years and stepbrother, Robert, aged 10 years. Robert Thornton Small, aged 41 years was a builders labourer and his wife, Elsie, 39 years was the catering manageress at the nearby Whitley Bay Ice Rink.

For many years, Michael simply did not see eye to eye with his stepfather – Robert, and a state of 'Cold War' existed between the pair. It was in fact believed that Robert had a particular hatred of his stepson, Michael, a hatred that was also reciprocal. Neighbours used to talk of bottle parties and hearing frequent arguments between Elsie and Robert. On Tuesday 16th March 1971, Michael was sitting at home with his stepfather, when his mother came home from work at the Ice Rink. Elsie did not speak to her husband, and after unusually eating supper on her own in the kitchen, went upstairs to bed. Michael could sense that a row was brewing, which was confirmed a few minutes later when his stepfather tried to force his way into the room where Elsie was sleeping. A short time later, an argument ensued between the couple, which ended up in the kitchen. The following morning, Michael noticed that the beds had been rearranged in such a way as to enable his stepfather to sleep in a single bed on his own in the small rear bedroom.

The Small family home, 37 Priory Avenue, Hillheads in 1971.

Michael was out of the house all day on Thursday 18th March 1971, and did not return until Midnight that day. His mother was not up, and his stepfather surprised him by preparing his supper for him, which was a very unusual occurrence. Michael then went to bed. The next morning, Friday 19th March 1971, Michael discovered that his mother had not been in the house all night. His stepfather appeared completely unconcerned. Michael became worried about the situation, so later that day he decided to hitch hike to his grandmother's house at Stoke on Trent to see if she had in fact gone there.

After spending a long weekend with his grandmother, and finding his mother was not there, he returned home to Priory Avenue, arriving there at 9am on the morning of Tuesday 23rd March 1971. The sight that confronted Michael was horrific.

On opening the front door, and walking into the front living room, he found his stepfather – Robert lying unconscious on the floor, breathing only in very shallow gasps, and frothing at the mouth. Michael noticed some pages of notepaper nearby, and on reading them he realised that something terrible had happened to his mother. Michael immediately ran upstairs to the large rear bedroom to look for his mother. The curtains were drawn shut and although the light was bad, he saw his stepsister, Jacqueline lying on the double bed, apparently asleep. He tried to wake her, but discovered that her shoulder was hard and cold. To his horror, he realised that she was dead and then rushed into the front bedroom where his younger brother, Robert normally slept. Michael saw Robert lying face down on a single bed, with his face buried into a pillow. When he turned Robert over, he could see that the child's face was blue, and he was also dead.

Frantic, Michael then ran into the small rear bedroom, where he saw Janet also lying face down on the bed, and realised that she too was dead. In a state of sheer panic, he left the house and managed to get a lift to Whitley Bay Police Station, which is about mile away, and reported what he had found. Accompanied by Detective Constable Jim Davis, they quickly returned to the house where Robert Thornton Small was still breathing very slowly on the floor of the living room. An ambulance was summoned, and he was taken immediately to Preston Hospital, where it was later confirmed that he had taken an overdose of tablets in an effort to take his own life.

Small was later transferred to the RVI at Newcastle, following kidney failure. Following a short search of the house, DC Davis found two empty tablet bottles and a loose capsule on the kitchen bench. The Police Surgeon, Dr. Wilf Phillips attended the scene, and certified that the children had been dead for many hours, and heavy ligature marks around their necks clearly indicated, even at this early stage that they had all been strangled.

At 9.30am, Detective Chief Inspector Hector Clark arrived at the house, and following a detailed examination of the scene found a piece of rope and a knotted tie on the landing floor. In the front bedroom, a leather belt was lying on the floor, and a second knotted tie was on the small bed. The bodies of all the children were still in position. Downstairs in the kitchen, it was noticed that a gas pipe had been sawn through, but fortunately, due to the position of the tap, no gas was escaping.

A letter, 10 pages long written by Robert Thornton Small, was found on the sideboard in the living room, which contained an account of how he had killed his wife. The letter however hardly made any reference to the children, but at this stage, there was still no sign of Elsie's body. A thorough search of the house continued, and a roll of carpet in a rear outhouse cupboard was examined, which was found to contain her body.

Following a post mortem, it was established that Elsie had suffered severe head injuries, and had also been subjected to manual strangulation, but the actual cause of death was found to be asphyxia, due to suffocation with a gag, i.e. a vest which had been stuffed into her mouth. Post Mortems on the children revealed that

Whitley Bay Police Station.

the cause of death in each case was asphyxia, due to strangulation by ligature.

The weapon used by Robert Thornton Small to inflict the head injuries on his wife, Elsie is believed to have been a piece of lead pipe, which he had discarded into a dustbin. The implement was never found. At 11.30am on Friday 26th March 1971, at Whitley Bay Courthouse, the coroner, Mr Brian Gallon opened and adjourned inquests whilst police investigations continued.

At 11am on Monday 29th March 1971, funerals of all the deceased were held at Whitley Bay Crematorium.

The following day, Small had made a recovery and was well enough to be interviewed by police, during which he admitted killing his wife, and writing the letter, before describing how he also killed the three children. On 8th April 1971, following his release from hospital, he was arrested, and subsequently charged with the murders of his wife, Elsie, and the three children, Janet, Robert and Jacqueline.

The motive for the murder of Elsie Small was jealousy, and was reflected in the letter written by Small where he believed that she was having an affair with a local man. Following the murder, it seemed reasonably clear that he could not bear the thought of his three children living in homes for the rest of their lives, and this somewhat unbalanced opinion resulted in him killing them.

Small was later convicted of the four murders and given a life sentence, of which he served 12 years imprisonment, latterly at Acklington Prison, Northumberland from where he was released in March 1983.

On Monday 11th April 1983, Robert Small perished when he was seen to jump from Whitley Bay Promenade into a stormy sea. The inquest returned a verdict of suicide

THE MONKSEATON SHOOTINGS

Sunday 30th April 1989 is a day that will probably never be forgotten in the history of Monkseaton Village. It was a bright sunny day, when at noon that day, reports flooded into the Northumbria Police Control Room of a man armed with a shotgun, who was indiscriminately shooting at residents and passers-by, in a quiet residential area of Monkseaton. The horrific events, which occurred on that day, received national publicity, which led Robert James Sartin to appear before North Shields Magistrates, charged with one murder, and a further seventeen attempted murders.

Robert James Sartin was a single, 22-year-old civil servant, who worked for the Department of Health and Social Security, at Blyth, Northumberland. He lived with his parents in a privately owned semi-detached house in Wentworth Gardens, at West Monkseaton. Robert Sartin's father was a member of a local gun club, who lawfully owned a shotgun and ammunition, which he kept at home. On Sunday 30th April 1989, Sartin's parents went to visit friends in Yorkshire, leaving Robert alone in the house. At around 11.40am that day, Sartin accessed his father's Baikal over & under double-barrelled shotgun, which he took along with a quantity of ammunition and put into his beige Ford Escort Motor Car, which he then drove to Pykerley Road, Monkseaton, and parked up. Sartin left his car, dressed completely in dark clothing, wearing a pair of dark sunglasses and armed with the loaded shotgun, he stalked the quiet tree lined streets of Monkseaton for around 20 minutes, deliberately and indiscriminately shooting at residents and passers-by.

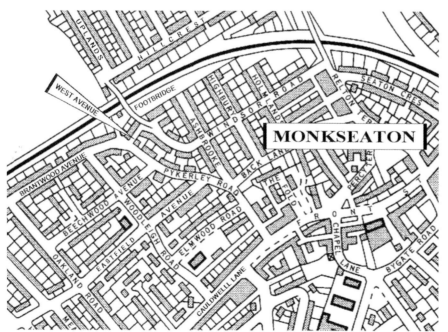

Police files established that Sartin walked more or less in a figure of eight pattern through the streets, walking firstly along Pykerley Road to West Avenue, into Windsor Road, Ashbrooke, back to Pykerley Road, into Eastfield Avenue, retraced his steps to Pykerley Road, then down Pykerley Road again into Brantwood Avenue, through a pedestrian footway into Northcote Avenue, then Beechwood Avenue, back to Pykerley Road where he had earlier parked his car. During his walk around these streets, Sartin shot a total of eighteen people which he encountered on the journey. It was later confirmed that he had no relationship whatsoever with any of the victims.

The terrifying morning ended when Sartin calmly got back into his car and drove off along Pykerley Road towards Brantwood Avenue. He then made his way towards the seafront and stopped in a public car park opposite the BriarDene Pub, where he was arrested by police. There was one fatality that day; Ken Mackintosh, a 41-year-old married man, who was also the Property Secretary of Monkseaton Methodist Church and had decided to walk home from the morning service to his home in Uplands, Monkseaton. Mr Mackintosh was walking along Windsor Road, towards West Avenue where a footbridge crosses the Metro railway line. At this time, Sartin was emerging from West Avenue, onto Windsor Road, where he saw Mr. Mackintosh approaching. At this point and from a very short distance, Sartin raised the weapon and fired both barrels of the shotgun directly at Mr. Mackintosh, killing him instantly.

Police by this time were inundated with calls and responding to each of the incidents as they were reported. PC Danny Herdman, of Whitley Bay Police Station was on duty that day in an unmarked police car and managed to get sight of Sartin's Ford Escort which he followed to a car park on the seafront at Whitley Bay, opposite the BriarDene pub. PC Herdman immediately arrested Sartin without a struggle. Sartin was found to be wearing a belt to which was attached a large sheath knife, and a bag containing a further five live shotgun cartridges.

During the course of the police enquiries that followed, it was established that Sartin had more than a passing interest in the occult, Satanism, horror and murder, and in fact whilst a pupil of Whitley Bay High School, he was counseled by a child psychiatrist in relation to his unnatural and unhealthy attitude and affinity to the occult. Sartin had a large collection of books on the subject, along with books relating to psychiatry, analysing murders and describing the symptoms of various psychiatric disorders, along with a scrapbook relating to murderers. He also had a comprehensive library of books, both fact and fictional, relating to the subject of mass murder.

On Monday 1st May 1989, Sartin was charged with the murder of Ken Mackintosh and appeared before North Shields Magistrates the following day, when he was remanded in custody to 30th May 1989. On this date, he was charged with seventeen offences of attempted murder, and was further remanded to 27th June 1989.

On Thursday 4th May 1989, the Deputy Coroner for North Tyneside, Mr Eric Armstrong opened the inquest into the death of Ken Mackintosh, and adjourned the proceedings until the finalisation of criminal proceedings. Robert Sartin eventually appeared at Durham Crown Court, but because of his unstable mental condition he was detained for life in a secure unit of a Psychiatric Institution.

A tree, planted in the small garden at the front of Monkseaton Methodist Church is accompanied by a simple plaque which reads: 'In Memory of Ken Mackintosh 1989'. Similarly, a nearby wooden cross bears a small plaque which reads; 'Donated by Colleagues, Friends and Neighbours, in memory of Ken Mackintosh'.

These tragic events which occurred in Monkseaton on the fateful day shocked and touched many people. The story is of course much more complex, therefore this account has been summarised and deliberately excludes a photograph of Robert Sartin in order to respect the wishes of Ken's family. Understandably, the horrors of 30th April 1989 continue to haunt the family, and I am very grateful to Ken's wife, Pam; daughter, Debbie and son, Roger for giving their blessing to this narrative which forms an important part of the history of Monkseaton Village.

In conclusion, we pay tribute to Ken, a British Telecom Engineer and long term resident of Monkseaton. Ken had been married to his wife; Pam for almost 18 years and was very much a family man who had a strong interest and commitment to Monkseaton Methodist Church. Supported by Pam, Ken assisted with many tasks to ensure the smooth day to day running of the church and was involved with a number of other church related groups, youth organisations and activities. He also served on the Whitley Bay Council of Churches as one of Monkseaton's representatives. Ken was a popular and dedicated man who was well liked, well respected and held in high regard by everyone who knew him.

To the Memory of Ken Mackintosh 1947-1989

HILLHEADS

It is useful to know that the area which is regularly referred to as 'Hillheads' is simply a corruption of its correct three word title, 'Whitley Hill Heads'. Travelling north east towards Whitley, Hill Heads Road was a continuation of 'Shields' Road – the main thoroughfare leading from Preston Township to Whitley Township and was little more than a road running through open fields with no housing other than a small handful of pit cottages which stood near the site of the present Railway Inn.

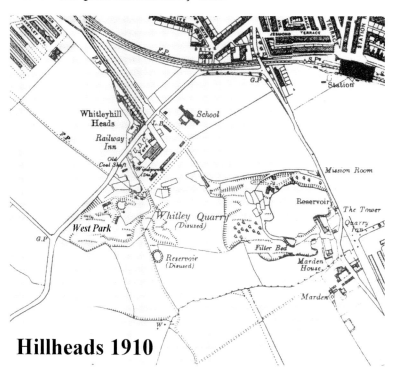

Hillheads 1910

The road ran adjacent to West Park on the right (*refer to page 65*), which formed the north-western boundary of Marden Limestone Quarry. This area is now occupied by the Ice Rink and cricket field and just beyond here was Whitley Colliery which in later years became the council yard and nearby abattoir until replaced by the present housing. The old colliery chimney was a landmark there for many years until it was demolished in 1953.

The old Monkseaton/North Shields waggonway which opened in 1811, crossed Hill Heads Road at a point very close to the present Kingsley Avenue, and ran through Marden Limestone Quarry, then parallel to the Broadway, into Spital Dene, terminating at the Low Lights staithes in North Shields. The waggonway which took coal from Whitley pits and limestone from Marden Quarry, closed in 1850. Originally, in 1861, the first passengers to and from Whitley, left or boarded the train for Newcastle at a halt called Whitley Hillheads. When the railway was re-aligned in 1882, the site became a marshalling yard with goods and coal sidings which remained here for many years.

In post-war years, perhaps two of the most well known local coal merchants operating from these sidings included Straughan's and Eric Capstick.

When the rails were eventually removed, the area was levelled and became a caravan storage facility with an adjoining small lorry park. Some small commercial units were also built along with a garage which was occupied by Colebrook and Burgess. The land was further developed in the 1980s with a large supermarket and accompanying car park.

In 1913 much of the land that was once occupied by the nearby Hill Heads Farm was sold, and quickly developed to accommodate a new Secondary School, which, when completed received its first pupils in September 1914. Originally called Whitley

A painting of Hill Heads Farm, c.1890, showing Whitley Colliery chimney to the right.

and Monkseaton High School for Boys and Whitley and Monkseaton High School for Girls, they became co-educational in 1937 and the name was changed to Whitley Grammar School in 1945.

In 1963, the school transferred to newly-built accommodation in Deneholm, and the building once again changed its status to Hillheads County Secondary School, and then owing to comprehensive reorganisation in 1973, to Marden Bridge Middle School

During the 1990s, further development took place with the construction of a multi-purpose Sports and Leisure Centre.

The first houses to be built at Hill Heads were laid out for Whitley Bay Urban District Council in 1913 when 38 homes were erected in Hotspur and Lovaine Avenue. This site had once been part of the old Whitley Colliery premises, and several years later, two of these houses were severely affected by subsidence due to underground mine workings and became so unsafe that they had to be demolished.

The Great War of 1914-1918 halted all further building work, but in the ten years which followed from 1919, the Hill Heads Estate of Kingsley, Priory, Dowling, Chestnut, Sycamore and Belvedere Avenues and The Nook were built. During that period, a total of 402 council houses were constructed.

The end of Whitley Colliery Chimney – 1953.

Much of the remaining land which adjoined Hill Heads to form the boundary with Marden Limestone Quarry, was adapted for recreational purposes and now accommodate Rockcliff Rugby Club, West Park Cricket Field, Whitley Bay Football Club, Hill Head Allotments and the Ice Rink as well as one of the longest established businesses; Whitley Bay Boarding Kennels.

These premises are situated to the rear of the Ice Rink and were first set up in 1926 by M & J Pearson where for many years they were always locally referred to as 'Pearson's Cat & Dog Shelter'. Over the years, the building has been extended and modernised to provide clean and safe accommodation facilities for the boarding of both dogs and cats and still runs under a family ownership.

An unusual advertisement taken from a 1920s Whitley Bay Guidebook illustrates the Holidays Information Bureau, with an address of 33 Dowling Avenue (Hill Heads) – a residential property. The main offices were situated in Torquay, Devon, but nothing else is known of the organisation. Presumably, the Dowling Avenue address was one of the local booking offices.

HILLHEADS SLAUGHTERHOUSE

During the latter part of the 1800s into the early 1900s, a slaughterhouse stood in the centre of Monkseaton Village and was situated on the corner of Front Street and Chapel Lane, on the site now occupied by No. 39 Front Street.

Slaughtering methods were crude, and when the building was eventually vacated, a site was secured to the south of the village at Whitley Hill Heads, opposite the old Railway Inn where an abattoir was built to the rear of the council yard and to the back of Hotspur Avenue.

This location was considered ideal, as cattle, sheep and pigs which were transported by train, usually arrived at the nearby railway sidings around 9.30pm in the evening, and after unloading, involved only a very short journey to the actual slaughterhouse which was situated to the rear of Hotspur Avenue and the adjoining council yard. Slaughtering took place in the late evening until around 1am in the morning.

The slaughtering methods used to kill the beasts in those days were crude and cruel and it is difficult to conceive that sheep were actually blown up by human breath to facilitate skinning.

The urban council to whom the slaughterhouse belonged, eventually introduced bylaws which fixed more civilised hours for killing, as well as insisting on several other requirements designed to protect public health and reduce the cruelty and suffering to the fated animals, which included a system of examining all carcasses before they left the slaughterhouse.

Looking west up Front Street in 1904. The Village Slaughterhouse is the single storey building to the left of the picture standing on the corner of Chapel Lane.

During this time, many of Whitley Bay's butchers had the reputation of obtaining first choice of the finest stock in the country for slaughter, and all the best beef came from bullocks and heifers. The butchers even ran their own insurance scheme to protect them from condemned carcasses.

Apparently in the twelve years leading up to the war, only two cows were recorded as being killed in the town for meat.

In 1940, Whitley Urban District Council took over the slaughtering of all animals on behalf of the Ministry of Food, and the Hillheads slaughterhouse then became the public abattoir serving nearly all the butchers in the surrounding areas which included Whitley Bay, Tynemouth and North Shields.

By the early 1950s, an average of 30,000 animals were being killed by controlled methods every year. Modern equipment such as electric saws and winches were introduced to replace the outdated hand-operated machinery. Spring loaded guns were used to stun sheep prior to killing and pigs were electrocuted rather than being shot. In later years, the council relinquished control of the abattoir, which was eventually taken over by the Whitley Bay Meat Supply Company.

Slaughtering continued for many years thereafter, and during the 1980s the Whitley Bay Meat Supply Company moved to modern hygienic and purpose built facilities at Burradon where slaughtering is now carried out using modern, humane and up to date methods.

WEST PARK, HILLHEADS

The area of land adjacent to the Ice Rink at Hillheads which is now used as a cricket and recreation field is known as West Park.

Originally forming the north-western section of the Magnesium Limestone Quarry at Marden, and also part of Hill Heads Farm, West Park was purchased by a Richard Heckels Nesbit around 1875 where he set up a steam brickworks.

Although in poor perspective, this picture dates to around 1880 and shows the brickworks at West Park from a position slightly to the south east of where the present Ice Rink stands. The trees on the 'horizon' are actually standing on Hill Heads Road and help to illustrate the depth of the quarry at this time.

At this time, Nesbit had also bought Bygate Farm in Monkseaton. He became a prominent member of Whitley Urban District Council, where alongside Alfred Styan, he became a pioneer builder in Whitley, and was responsible for much of the construction work on Albany Gardens, Clarence Crescent, Edwards Road, The Esplanade, Laburnum Avenue, Station Road, and Mafeking Street (later renamed as Fern Avenue).

Many of the bricks which were manufactured at Hillheads were used in the construction of these houses. By 1889, the brickworks at Hillheads were exhausted, so Nesbit ceased operations and landscaped the entire area in order to create West Park where he resided until his death in 1911. West Park was then sold to Mr. George Steel, a Florist and Nurseryman who owned gardens in Park View, Whitley Bay.

George Steel utilised West Park as Market Gardens where he built greenhouses, stables and outbuildings, as well as making a vast number of improvements to the land. West Park at this time was a deep quarry with steep sides, approximately 90 feet below the level of the adjacent Hill Heads Road with a row of four cottages at the bottom. There were 134 wood-

When the brickworks closed, the cottages remained and West Park was landscaped to create nursery gardens. Hill Heads Road is visible in the background.

fronted clay steps descending from the main road into the quarry, terminating at the rear of the houses.

George Steel and his family took up residence in Nesbits former house at No.1 West Park (the end house on the right of the picture on the bottom of page 65) and he rented out the remaining three houses. Steel retained ownership of West Park until 1924, when Whitley Urban District Council placed a compulsory purchase notice on the land, forcing him to move out shortly afterwards.

When the order took effect, the cottages were demolished and the council began infilling with thousands of tons of earth and rubble, commencing at the western edge of the land where, by 1931, controlled refuse tipping was also in progress. Eventually, the original 90 foot deep quarry/park was raised to its present height, grassed over and landscaped to become the present cricket field.

Richard Heckels Nesbit and his wife outside No. 1 West Park, Hillheads c.1900.

West Park in 1931 during controlled refuse tipping. The houses in the distance are on the corner of Hill Heads Road and show Sycamore and Chestnut Avenue. The tall chimney to the right was the old Whitley Colliery chimney which was a landmark for many years and stood in what became the Urban District Council Yard. It was demolished in 1953.

MARDEN QUARRY

Dating back to the mid 1600s, magnesium limestone was quarried at Marden and Hill Heads for a period of almost 200 years.

Situated towards the northern extremity of Hill Heads, the quarry represents virtually the only exposure of magnesium limestone north of the River Tyne. The original quarry area occupied the land between the present Ice Rink on Hill Heads Road and Shaftesbury Crescent forming the boundary with Marden Estate, and bordering Marden Road South and the Broadway to the East.

Large quantities of limestone was transported via a waggonway and shipped abroad from loading staithes at North Shields.

When the limestone workings ceased towards the mid 1800s, Marden Reservoir was formed, and overseen by the

Marden Farm, c.1912.

North Shields and Tynemouth Water Company while much of the quarry land to the west became detached to become West Park *(see separate section)*. The remaining area then adopted the name of 'Marden Quarry' because of its close proximity to Marden Farm and Cottages which stood a short distance to the south adjacent to the original Broadway.

A small group of houses known as 'New Whitley' were situated on the southern edge of the quarry close to Marden. It is unclear whether the cottages were originally connected with quarrymen or workers at the limestone quarry, but locally they were often colourfully referred to as 'Fiddler's Green'.

Marden Tower, c.1947.

A stone tower, which stood on Marden Road for many years, was originally built as quarry offices, and it is understood that it may also have been used as a powder and explosives store.

The tower stood as a landmark for many years, until it was demolished in 1965 along with the cottages at New Whitley.

Converted and landscaped to become an informal

New Whitley or 'Fiddlers Green', c. 1950.

nature park, Marden Quarry opened in 1977 as a Nature Reserve and was awarded Local Nature Reserve Status in the summer of 2005.

Marden Road South and The Broadway which run adjacent to the eastern edge of the quarry were widened and straightened during the 1920s however evidence still exists of the original curved Broadway route which can still be seen outside the present entrance to Marden Quarry. It runs past the gates of Marden House adjoining the quarry and now serves as an access road to feed Marden Farm Estate.

Prior to the 1920s, the route of the original Broadway between Tynemouth and Whitley ran past the entrance to Marden House and Quarry. This section of road is still in evidence today.

The first Quarry Inn dates from around 1854 and stood at the south-eastern extremity of Hill Heads at its boundary with Marden. It was situated on the west side of the old Broadway directly next to the entrance to Marden Quarry.

The first Quarry Inn in 1914. Marden House is to the extreme left and the curvature of the original Broadway is also evident.

In 1922, the Broadway was re-aligned and straightened, thus bypassing the old inn, which was demolished a few years later.

In 1927, after re-alignment of the new Broadway Road, the second Quarry Inn was commissioned, and construction work started during this year.

The inn was built on the opposite side of the road at the junction with Marden Road South and Burnside Road, almost directly opposite where the former inn stood.

The Broadway as seen from Marden Tower, during the early 1920s. The view along this once winding road looks south towards Tynemouth, with Marden Farm visible in the distance. The area of land to the left is now occupied by housing.

Marden Quarry when it was a reservoir. Marden Tower is clearly visible in the background, as are the buildings comprising 'New Whitley'.

MISCELLANEOUS
MONKSEATON AIR RAIDS

During the Second World War, Monkseaton encountered its share of wartime bombing raids, and in line with other parts of the country, suffered a number of casualties. Interestingly, no Council Houses in the area were destroyed during any Air Raids.

The following list is an overview of all the recorded Air Raids which occurred within the village environs.

As most Air Raids took place overnight, bombings may have continued into the following day and therefore some of the dates shown below may need to be adjusted accordingly.

22/6/40: Between 00.30hrs and 01.00hrs – Bomb damage was caused at Fair Green & Thorntree Drive, West Monkseaton.

6/7/40 03.00hrs: Air raids took place over Monkseaton.

8/7/40: Bombing to western end of Thorntree Drive, Dickies Holm Farm and adjacent Railway Line.

2/8/40: Incendiary bombs fell close to Beverley Park.

8/8/40: Incendiary bombs fell near Closefield Grove, and adjacent fields of Seatonville Estate.

An advert showing some of the furnishings you could have in your air raid shelter.

A gas mask and its cardboard box. Millions of respirators were issued as it was believed the Germans would use gas against civilians.

29/8/40 23.00hrs: A high explosive bomb fell to the rear of the Robin Hood Public House, Murton Village causing damage to window panes and surrounding properties. Four high explosive bombs fell in fields at Murton Village (two at North Farm and two at East Farm), causing only crater damage.

04.00hrs: Eleven high explosive and twenty incendiary bombs fell in Monkseaton Village in the Fold area, plus one unexploded device at No. 8 Lyndhurst Road. Five houses and four shops were completely demolished. No. 17 Roseberry Terrace received a direct hit causing two fatalities: Robert Brunton aged 23 years and his brother Richard aged 19 years. Other occupants of the house had sheltered in a cupboard under stairs and suffered only shock but had to be extracted from the wreckage. The old stone chapel on Chapel Lane received a direct hit and was totally destroyed. A bomb fell in Ivanhoe, followed by four high explosive bombs which also fell in fields to the west of Red House Farm.

10/4/41: A widespread cluster of over 360 incendiary bombs were dropped over Monkseaton, most of which fell in the area of Hillheads Estate between Sycamore and Kingsley Avenue. Some of these incendiaries caused fires to trains in sidings at Monkseaton Station and an ambulance travelling nearby was hit. At 04.26hrs a First Aid Post in Holmlands was hit resulting in 2 fatalities.

6/5/41: A total of 3 high explosive and 15 incendiary bombs fell on Well Lane, north east of Murton Village.

11/7/41: Bombs fell in the area of Paignton Avenue, Wembley Avenue, Lena Avenue and Melbourne Crescent.

22/7/41: Bombs landed in fields to the rear of Newsteads Farm.

10/8/41: Incendiary bombs fell in the Beverley Road, Haig Avenue and Hill Heads Road area.

30/9/41: One bomb fell in a field at Dickies Holm Farm, West Monkseaton.

1/10/41: Bombs fell in fields to the west of Shields Road on the site of Cherrytree Gardens, Baytree Gardens and Churchill Avenue.

8/12/41: Four fatalities occurred when a bomb hit No. 12 Swinbourne Gardens, Monkseaton completely destroying it. The occupants of the premises were William Hughes-Jones aged 59 years, his wife, Margaret, aged 55 years; son William, aged 27 years and daughter Brenda, aged 15 years. Houses in nearby Kings Road and Tynedale Avenue also suffered damage. During the same air raid, a bomb also fell on the railway sidings to the rear of Kingsley Avenue.

29/12/41: Four high explosive bombs landed in outlying fields of Red House Farm.

11/10/42: Bombing occurred next to Woodleigh Road and Eastfield Avenue, and a 1000lb device destroyed ten houses and caused severe damage to a further seventy properties (twenty irreparably). One person was killed and two were seriously injured. Another bomb fell on Cauldwell Close and more landed in fields to the rear Newsteads Farm.

14/12/42: Incendiary bombs fell in fields just east of Shields Road (on what is now the Foxhunters Trading Estate). The Avenue Branch Railway Line was hit and parts of Hartley Avenue suffered blast damage.

22/3/43: Seven high explosive and five incendiaries fell in fields to north of Rake House Farm.

The official End of War Report compiled by Sir Arthur Lambert (North Regional Commissioner) recorded the following casualties in the Whitley Bay and Monkseaton UDC area: 34 Deaths
                43 Injured/Hospitalised
                184 Slight or Minor Injuries

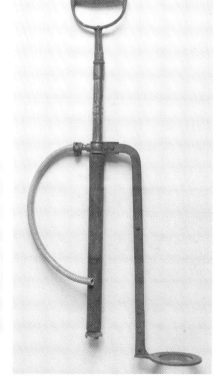

Two pieces of equipment used in air raids.

Right: An ARP (Air Raid Precautions) rattle or crake – used to sound alarm. After the war these rattle were often seen at football grounds with fans using them to cheer on their team.

Far right: A stirrup pump used to put out fires caused by incendiary bombs.

Ten Houses were destroyed when a 1000lb bomb fell close to St Andrew's Church on 11th October 1942.

On 11th October 1942 a massive bomb caused devastation to the area of Woodleigh Road and Eastfield Avenue. Several houses were destroyed and nearby St Peter's Church suffered significant damage.

Damage to a number of properties occurred in The Fold during a heavy bombing raid which took place on 29th August 1940. The houses were later demolished and the site was cleared to accommodate the present flats which were built on the vacant land in 1955. Rosebery Court Sheltered Housing which was built in the late 1960s now

occupies the area visible in the foreground. The row of terraced houses to the background are numbered 9 to 19 The Fold and still exist.

Above: This map is for illustrative purposes only, in order to show those areas affected by the air raids, as not all streets shown on the map had been built at the time of the bombings. (Reproduced from the 1966 Ordnance Survey map with the kind permission of the Ordnance Survey.)

Right: 12 Swinbourne Gardens was rebuilt.

EXTRACTS FROM EARLY MONKSEATON DIRECTORIES

This extract, taken from Kelly's Directory of Northumberland shows the Private Residents and Commercial Businesses in Monkseaton during 1902.

PRIVATE RESIDENTS

Allan Jas. M. The Poplars, Marine Avenue
Allen John Parnell, Rokeby, Marine Avenue
Arkwright Bernard, The Willows, Marine Avenue
Barber George Best, Grasmere
Bateson Mrs. Rock Cottage
Bell Thos. Summerleigh, Marine Avenue
Blackburn Burdus Bedford, Daisyville, Marine Avenue
Brown John Williamson, jun. Grosvenor House
Charlton Joseph, 3 Victoria Place
Charlton Mrs. Carlton Ho. Marine Avenue
Christie Mrs. Rosebank, Marine Avenue
Clark Hy. Inglehurst, Osborne Gardens
Crawford Fredk. Hazelhurst, Marine Avenue
Creigh John, Elmfield, Marine Avenue
Davidson Robert
Edger Chas. H. Burnwood. Osborne Gardens
Elliott Mrs. Monkseaton House
Elliott Thomas William J.P. The Cottage
Fairbairn Jn. Denbigh, Osborne Gardens
Falconar Miss, North Cottage
Fenwick John, Shellacres, Marine Avenue
Glaholm George, Hawthorns, Osborne Gardens
Green Thomas, West House

Grey Mrs. Front Street
Hamsen Nicholaus, Claremont, Osborne Gardens
Haswell Francis R. N. Caldwell House
Hinton Norman Crofton, Glendyn
Huntley Daniel Robert, Island View, Marine Avenue
Jardine Edward Amory, Marine Avenue
Lawson James, Marine Avenue
Lockyer Mrs, Marine House
Mason Frederick, Saville Ho. Marine Avenue
Melross Gilbert G. Nithsdale, Marine Avenue
Milburn Mrs. Front Street
Monkhouse Frederick, Myrtleville, Marine Avenue
Mullen Henry J.
Nicholls Mrs. Port-a-Shee, Marine Avenue
Potts John Atkinson, Kelvinhoe, Marine Avenue
Potts Mrs. Clayton House
Proctor Wm. Hy. Annadale, Marine Avenue
Reed Matthew, Etherley, Osborne Gardens
Richardson Mrs. Front Street
Robson John, 8 Osborne Gardens
Robson Joseph Tinn, Beetholme, Osborne Gardens
Smith John Addison, Sunnyside, Marine Avenue

Looking East on Marine Avenue, c.1906. The corner of Park Road is in the distance.

Smith Roger Bickerton, Front Street
Storey Henry, Jessamine House
Thompson George Dobson, Ashleigh,
    Marine Avenue
Thorburn Miss, Eskdale, Osborne Gardens
Wait Miss, West House
Watson George, Bertlea, Marine Avenue
Weightman Francis Elliott, Denholm,
    Osborne Gardens
Williams Charles, Glencarn, Marine Avenue
Wilson Henry, Bromley Place
Wright Robert, 11 Osborne Gardens

COMMERCIAL

Anderson Oscar E. (Master Mariner)
Appleby John, (Farmer)
    South West Farm
Bywater Thomas, (Market Gardener)
    Dickies Holm
Charlton Thomas, (Market Gardener)
    Dickies Holm
Davidson Robert, (Assistant Overseer for
    Preston & Monkseaton and Registrar of
    Births & Deaths, Whitley Sub-district)
    Rose Cottage
Davidson Thomas, (Blacksmith)
Davidson William Tweddell, (Cartwright &
    Joiner)

Dobinson Josiah & Miss Jane, (Farmers)
    Seatonville Farm
Dryden Robert, (Builder & Farmer)
Dunn Charles, (Farmer)
    Red House Farm
Fogg Geo. (Farmer)
    Burnt House Farm
Gibson Thomas S. (Manager)
    Ye Olde Monkseaton Arms P.H.
Hills William, Black Horse P.H.
Nelless John, (Farmer)
    East Farm
Nicholson Henry, (Farmer)
Northumberland Brewery Co,
    (Emra Holmes, Jun. Manager; John Geo.
    Wood, Sec.) Monkseaton Brewery
Potts Matthew, (Farmer)
    West Farm Dairy
Ritchie Nichol, (Builder)
    Rosecroft, Marine Avenue
Robson Christopher, (Grocer)
    see Scott & Robson
Sanderson Elizabeth Mrs., (Laundress)
Scott & Robson, (Grocers)
    7 Percy Terrace
Smith Roger, (Threshing Machine Owner)
    Front Street
Younger Edward, Ship Inn

Monkseaton

Marine Avenue — Holywell Avenue — Black Horse & Ship Inns & Coronation Row — Briar Dene Golf Links — The Fold, 1893 — Monkseaton Village, With Brewery & Monkseaton Arms — Blacksmith's Shop, 1893

This extract, taken from Kelly's Directory of Northumberland shows the Private Residents and Commercial Businesses in Monkseaton during 1925

PRIVATE RESIDENTS

Adams John Garfield, 29 Queen's Road
Adamson Reginald, 29 Holywell Avenue
Addison Mrs. 37 Queen's Road
Aitken Thomas, 73 Queen's Road
Alcock Henry William, 7 The Avenue
Alderson Mrs. 37 Hawthorn Gardens
Allan John, Eskdale, Osborne Gardens
Allen Jas. Thompson, 8 Elmwood Road
Allen Thomas, 2 Osborne Gardens
Allison Herbert, 57 Queen's Road
Anderson Arth. S. 9 Kensington Gardens
Anderson Edward Lowry, 18 Front Street
Arlison Christr. 4 Swinbourne Gardens
Askquith Sidney James, 3 Tynedale Ave
Atkinson Harry, Southwood, Claremont
    Gardens
Austin William Robt.13 Cromer Gardens
Baker Alfred, 71 Holywell Avenue
Baker Hubert Henry, 92 Marine Avenue
Baldwin Christopher E., J.P. 32 Holywell
    Avenue
Ballard Maxwell, 5 Tynedale Avenue
Balls Capt. Arthur C. 41 Holywell Avenue
Barclay Matthew Oswald, 7 Holywell Avenue
Barker Harry B. 23 St. George's Crescent
Barnes Wm. N. 1 Bournemouth Gardens
Barnett Wm. Geo. 62 Marine Avenue
Barnfather Fred, 48 Queen's Road
Barr Alfred James, 3 The Avenue
Baston Walter B.Sc. 9 Hawthorn Gardens

Bates George Henry, North End, Bygate Road
Batey Frank, 83 Queen's Road
Beale Lt.-Col. Henry, 86 Marine Avenue
Beevers Thomas, 34 Holywell Avenue
Bell Jonathan, 12 Claremont Gardens
Bell Mrs. 73 Marine Avenue
Bell Robert, 45 Holywell Avenue
Bell William Surtees, 14 Beech Grove
Bellis Alfred Hawker, 45 Queen's Road
Bertram Ernest, 67 Queen's Road
Besley Charles Holland, 53 Queen's Road
Biggan Mrs. Braemar, Beverley Road
Birkett Draycot Delegarde, Brockenhurst,
    Osborne Gardens
Black Alex, Nicoll, 43 Hawthorn Gardens
Black Robert, 58 Marine Avenue
Blackburn Robert L. 6 St. George's Crescent
Blackburn Thos. 4 St. George's Crescent
Bonson Clement, 85 Holywell Avenue
Borck Mrs. 113 Marine Avenue
Borland Mrs. 52 Queen's Road
Bowes Proctor, 27 Holywell Avenue
Bradford George O. 46 Marine Avenue
Bradley Walt. Fredk. 12 Beverley Road
Braithwaite Robt. F. 60 Ventnor Gardens
Brewer Osmond, 60 Marine Avenue
Briggs Jsph. Hy. 12 Beverley Park
Brooks Chas. Montague, 3o Beverley Road
Brown Harry Austine, 3 Beverley Park
Brown Hugh M. 12 Elmwood Road

Queens Road looking North from Tynedale Avenue, c. 1940. The gabled houses in the distance are Nos. 81 and 83 Queens Road.

Balmoral Gardens, looking east from the junction with Queens Road, c.1920.

Brown Mrs. E. 59 Front Street
Brown Richd. Wm. 81 Holywell Avenue
Brunskill William, 12 Beech Grove
Bryan Mark V. 7 St. George's Crescent
Bullock Mrs. 3 Elmwood Road
Burgess William, 33 Hawthorn Gardens
Burn John T.C. 8 Claremont Gardens
Burnside Wilfred M. 71 Queen's Road
Burrow William O. Rosemount, Eastfield
    Avenue
Burton Thos. Mundy, 4 The Gardens
Byers Herbert, 14 Claremont Gardens
Cadogen Archibald, 3 Swinbourne Gardens
Campbell William, 4 Beverley Road
Capill Robt. 33 Holywell Avenue
Caris Athol Kennedy, 51 Queen's Road
Cartwright Alfred Birks, 50 Holywell Avenue
Castlehow Wm. Hy. 63 Holywell Avenue
Caunt George W. 50 Queen's Road
Chappey Robert, Murtonroyde, Sanderson
    Road
Charlton Wm. Hy. 24 The Gardens
Chaytor Mrs. 39 Queen's Road
Chicken William Thomas, 9 Holywell
    Avenue
Chisholm Thos. M. 19 St. George's Crescent
Chrisp Thomas. 8 Kensington Gardens
Christie Misses, 96 Marine Avenue
Christopher Richard, 105 Marine Avenue
Clark Mrs. 10 Hawthorn Gardens
Clephem Guy, 16 Front Street
Coates John Robson, 7 Hawthorn Gardens
Coldwell John, Roslyn Cottage, The Grove
Cole Herbt. W. Clevedon, Eastfield Avenue
Connell Edwin James, 19 Queen's Road
Cook Frederick, 46 Holywell Avenue
Coull William, 21 The Gardens

Cowan Edward, 6 The Avenue
Cowen Henry W. 53 Holywell Avenue
Crossling Edward, 5 King's Road
Cullen Sidney, 73 Eastbourne Gardens
Cunningham William M.B. Coquet House,
    Marine Avenue
Curtis Walter, 53 Marine Avenue
Cusworth James, 75 Queen's Road
Dale Robert, 72 Holywell Avenue
Davison Alfred William, Carlton Villa,
    Marine Avenue
Davison Bartholomew, 5 St. George's Crescent
Davison Henry, 31 Holywell Avenue
Dickinson Sidney H. 13 The Gardens
Dickinson Thos. Allan, 38 Holywell Avenue
Dickinson William, West House, Pykerley
    Road
Dix Chas. Marshall, 13 Kenilworth Road
Dixon Herbt. 87 Marine Avenue
Dixon Mrs. 25 Queen's Road
Dixon Theodore Geo. 4 Abbotsford Park
Dobson Harry, 7 Swinbourne Gardens
Dobson Joseph. St. Margaret's Lodge.
    Marine Avenue
Dodds Godfrey William, Rest Harrow,
    The Grove
Douglas Maj. Sir James Stewart bart.
    Clifton House. Marine Avenue
Douthwaite Alfred, 1 Holywell Avenue
Dowsett James Henry, 14 Kensington
    Gardens
Dowzer Thomas M.C. F.R.C.S. 54 Marine Ave
Duncan Richard W. 61 Queen's Road
Dyy Capt. William Henry D. Fernlea, King's
    Road
Edmondson Robert Robson, 20 St. George's
    Crescent

Ely William, 48 Holywell Avenue
Fail Henry, 1 Kensington Gardens
Falconar Miss, 33 Front Street
Farish Thomas S. 5 Holywell Avenue
Farrow Tom. 13 Beverley Park
Fawcett Robert, 28 Cliftonville Gardens
Fell Robert, 1 Windsor Gardens
Ferguson James, 6 Beverley Road
Ferry Miss. 26 The Gardens
Flint James Anderson, 58 Queen's Road
Forgie John, 64 Queen's Road
Forrest John J. 15 Kensington Gardens
Forster Jn. Chas. 5 Swinbourne Gardens
Forster John Hall. 13 Queen's Road
Foster Harry, 2 Clovelly Gardens
Fowkes William H. 49 Marine Avenue
Franey Wm. Goulding, 11 Cromer Gardens
French Mrs. Thornhill, The Grove
Fry Henry Lorenz, 6 Elmwood Road
Fryer Jn. M. Stonevhurst, Deneholm
Futers Thomas C. 103 Marine Avenue
Gardner David, 13 Bournemouth Gardens
Gardner Joseph, 12 Kensington Gardens
Gedye William Frank, 101 Marine Avenue
Gibb James, 8 Holywell Avenue
Gibb Mrs. 16 Kensington Gardens
Gibberson John Wm. 7 Tynedale Avenue
Gibson Mrs. 8 Hawthorn Gardens
Gibson Mrs, 30 Holywell Avenue
Gilhespie Charles, 24 St. George's Crescent
Gilhespy Robert, 62 Holywell Avenue
Gill Edward, Greta Ho. Ventnor Gardens
Gilliat Albert E. 7 Claremont Gardens
Gofton James E. 19 Deneholm
Gofton Joseph A. 2 West Avenue
Gofton Richard A. 4 Uplands

Graham Robert, 1 Swinbourne Gardens
Gray Mrs. 56 Queen's Road
Gray Samuel Edwd. 44 Holywell Avenue
Gregory Mrs. 50 Queen's Road
Grey Frank, Chaddesden, Front Street
Grieve Thos. Myrtleville, Marine Avenue
Hadeway Stanley, 7 Queen's Road
Hails Mrs. 107 Marine Avenue
Hall Thomas, 39 Holywell Avenue
Hammond Fredk. 8 Swinbourne Gardens
Harbottle John, 32 St. George's Crescent
Harbottle Mrs. 9 Cromer Gardens
Harbottle William C. M 16 St.George's
    Crescent
Harding Jas. 34 Beverley Road
Hardy Alfd. 115 Marine Avenue
Harle William, 5 Kensington Gardens
Harrison Mrs. A. H. 11 The Gardens
Hastings Arthur Linay, 12 The Gardens
Hedley John, 1 The Avenue
Henderson Thomas E. Denbigh,
    Osborne Gardens
Henderson William S. 23 The Gardens
Heslop E. Brinton, Aldersyde, Marine Avenue
Heslop Thomas, 11 Front Street
Heywood John, 15 Queen's Road
Hindson Frank, 9 Beverley Park
Hinton Norman Crofton, 60 Holywell Avenue
Hogg William, 3 The Gardens
Holmes Fred, 89 Marine Avenue
Hope Geo. 64 Marine Avenue
Hope James, 16 Queen's Road
Hope John, 12 St. George's Crescent
Hope John Purves, 5 The Avenue
Hope John Robt. 14 Beverley Road
Horsfall William, 12 Claremont Gardens

This 1916 view of Ilfracombe Gardens looks south from the junction with Kew Gardens. Looking along the street from right to left, the visible terraced houses in the foreground are numbers 27-13.

Claremont Gardens, c.1920, looking north from Ilfracombe Gardens near to the junction with Bournemouth Gardens. The opposing houses are Nos. 104, 106 and 108 Ilfracombe Gardens.

Hough Edward P. 18 Claremont Gardens
Hoyde Sidney, 56 Marine Avenue
Hudson Percv A. 11 Bournemouth Gardens
Hunter Leslie E. 55 Holywell Avenue
Hunter Mrs. 62 Queen's Road
Huntingdon Charles, 16 Elmwood Road
Hutchinson Percy, 73 Holywell Avenue
Hutton John, 18 Beverley Road
Hyde Misses, 26 St. George's Crescent
Innes William, 3 Bournemouth Gardens
Ivison George Christopher, 17 Kensington
  Gardens
Jackson Henry John, Eastfield House,
  Eastfield Avenue
James Charles Atkinson, Grosvenor House,
  Front Street
Keenlevside Alfred, 10 Claremont Gardens
Kemp Donald. 95 Marine Avenue
Kennedy Capt. A, Keena, 16 Claremont
  Gardens
Kirsop David M. 13 Hawthorn Gardens
Kirtley William, 35 Holywell Avenue
Kitchen Hy. 77 Queen's Road
Knott Fred. 16 Holywell Avenue
Knox Thomas, 32 Beverley Road
Laidlaw Charles Wm. 40 King's Road
Laird Hy. Laurelwood, Holywell Avenue
Latham Albert Geo. 6 Holvwell Avenue
Lawson Joseph, Windholt, The Grove
Leathard Arth. Wm. 41 Marine Avenue
Lee James, 9 The Gardens
Leiper James Alexander M.B. 76 Marine
  Avenue
Levy Mrs. 1 Clovelly Gardens
Lewis Capt. William Henry, Aberfeld,
  Osborne Gardens
Liddell Mrs. 61 Holywell Avenue
Liddle Thomas N. 36 The Gardens

Lidstrom Alfred Percy, 59 Holywell Avenue
Lindsay Misses, 2 The Avenue
Linnel John G. 27 St. George's Crescent
Lister Mrs. Glenholme, Beverley Road
Lockerby Samuel, 41 Queen's Road
Longhurst Jsph. Jas. 4 Claremont Gardens
Lonie James, 3 Claremont Gardens
McAuslan William, 6 Hawthorn Gardens
Macaulay John William, Oakleigh,
  Kenilworth Road
McCaw Newton, 35 Queen's Road
Macdonald Charles A. 11 St.George's Crescent
McDonald John Wm. 56 Holywell Avenue
McDonald William, 22 Marine Avenue
McDowall Andrew L. 23 Hawthorn Gardens
McGlashan Geo. D. 24 Marine Avenue
Macgregor Wm. Low, 44 Holywell Avenue
McIlvenna James G. 15 St. George's Crescent
Mackay Francis W. 9 Queen's Road
MacKendreck Geo. H. 60 Queen's Road
McKendrick James, Brizlee, Beverley Road
McKenna Mrs. 41 Hawthorn Gardens
Mackinlay Norman Blackwood L.D.S. Edin.
  56 Marine Avenue
McMurtrie Radburne Angus, 48 Marine
  Avenue
McQuillen Wm. 30 St. George's Crescent
Madsen Frederick, 9 Claremont Gardens
Mard John hy. 11 Kensington Gardens
Marr John George, 2 Holywell Avenue
Marshall Fdk.65 Holywell Avenue
Marshall Mrs. F. C. 44 Marine Avenue
Marshall Mrs. Frank, Burnwood,
  Osborne Gardens
May Frank, 54 Queen's Road
Mayhew George, 57 Marine Avenue
Meikle Mrs. 93 Marine Avenue
Meikle William, 4 Holywell Avenue

Milburn Miss, 47 Queen's Road
Miller Miss, 63 Marine Avenue
Milne James, 72 Queen's Road
Mills Miss, 25 Hawthorn Gardens
Mitchell Jas. W. 40 St. George's Crescent
Montgomery Henry, 14 Front Street
More Andrew, 63 Queen's Road
Morgan Esmond T. 26 Beverley Road
Morris James P. 2 Kensington Gardens
Morrison William J. 18 Holywell Avenue
Morton John, 91 Cliftonville Gardens
Mountain Bertram H. 17 Cromer Gardens
Muckle Mark, Bygate Road
Mulcester Miss, 77 Holywell Avenue
Murdoch George, 31 Queen's Road
Nevin Edward, 4 Clovelly Gardens
Newton Mrs. 15 Hawthorn Gardens
Newton Mrs. 19 The Gardens
Nicholson John Gibb M.A., M.B. Shellacres,
    Marine Avenue
Noble James, 36 Beverley Road
Osborn Capt. Wm. Edwd. 5 Front Street
Oxnard Richard, 6 Beech Grove
Oxtoby Charles R. 55 Queen's Road
Pace Robert, 13 St. George's Crescent
Palmer Charles Douglas, 3 Holywell Avenue
Palmer Mrs. 5 Bournemouth Gardens
Parker Thomas, 33 St. George's Crescent
Parker Walter R. 75 Holywell Avenue
Parkin Richard, 7 Kensington Gardens
Parry William Hugh, 24 Beverley Road
Paterson Hugh, 43 Queen's Road
Paterson Keith, 25 St. George's Crescent
Patterson James B., M.D. 52 Marine Avenue

Paul Joseph Robert, 6 Beverley Park
Peacock Colin, 2 Beverley Road
Pearson Rev. John George (Wesleyan
    Methodist) 25 Bournemouth Gardens
Pescod Samuel, 13 Kensington Gardens
Peterson Fredk. Wm. 2 Beverley Park
Peterson Knud, 19 Bournemouth Gardens
Philipson George, 21 Hawthorn Gardens
Phillips Eric Betson, 24 Tynedale Avenue
Pickering Edwd. 3 Swinbourne Gardens
Potts John Atkinson, 11 Queen's Road
Potts John Francis, 29 Hawthorn Gardens
Potts Thomas Arthur, 21 Front Street
Pratt Rev. Henry (Primitive Methodist),
    27 Hawthorn Gardens
Price Walter Henry L.D.S. Cartmel, Front
    Street
Pringle James, 20 Claremont Gardens
Proctor Mrs. 47 Holywell Avenue
Proud Benjamin, 21 St. George's Crescent
Pye Walter Hy. 3 St. George's Crescent
Raine Henry Arthur, 3 Hawthorn Gardens
Readhead Thos. D. 11 Hawthorn Gardens
Reay James, 6 Kensington Gardens
Ridley Alfd. 14 The Gardens
Ridley George, 85 Eastbourne Gardens
Ridley Mrs. 1 The Gardens
Rimer Richd. Cowley, 10 Elmwood Road
Ritchie John, Cromlea, Cromer Gardens
Roberts Robert George, 4 Beverley Park
Robertson Jas. Denholm, Osborne Gardens
Robinson Arthur William, 8 St. George's
    Crescent
Robinson Johnson, 74 Marine Avenue

Marine Avenue in 1904. The signals for the railway crossing are evident in the distance.
The larger houses visible in the foreground are numbers 115 and 117 Marine Avenue.

Front Street, looking west from Monkseaton Railway Bridge.

Robinson Sydney, 81 Queen's Road
Robinson William Albert, 14 St. George's
    Crescent
Robson Arthur, 7 The Gardens
Robson Edmund John, Beaufront,
    Dene Crescent
Robson George Foxton, 7 Beverley Park
Robson Herbert Thomas, Henley, The Grove
Robson John P. 43 Holywell Avenue
Robson Joseph Tinn, Beetholme,
    Osborne Gardens
Robson Mrs. J. S. 88 Marine Avenue
Rogers Bowman I. 69 Holywell Avenue
Rogers James, 30 The Gardens
Rose Donald, 27 Queen's Road
Rosevear Hbt.T. 4 Bournemouth Gardens
Ross Thomas, 28 St. George's Crescent
Roxborgh Allan B. 83 Holywell Avenue
Ruddock Mrs. Staward
Rutherford William, 4 The Avenue
Ryder William Henry, The Lodge,
    Osborne Gardens
Saint Henry B. 29 Holywell Avenue
Sanderson Edward, 8 Beverley Park
Saul Joseph, 51 Holywell Avenue
Scott James Charles, 32 The Gardens
Seed Reginald, 17 Queen's Road
Sharpe Fredk.Hrbt. 5 Claremont Gardens
Shaw Edwin, 2 Evesham Gardens
Shearston Jsph. Allan, 14 Elmwood Road
Sherett Thomas R. 17 Hawthorn Gardens
Shield Robt. 70 Queen's Road
Shields Thomas, 65 Marine Avenue
Shimmin Robert Charles, 6 Claremont
    Gardens
Short William, 17 The Gardens

Shorthouse Ronald G. 17 Bournemouth
    Gardens
Simpson John, Follonsley, Hawthorn Gardens
Simpson William Thomas, Weetwood,
    Dene Crescent
Slack John N., L.D.S. 80 Marine Avenue
Sloan William James, 37 Holywell Avenue
Small John Barwick, 65 Queen's Road
Smee Wm.Hy. 1 Eastfield Avenue
Smirk Fdk. Wm. 39 Hawthorn Gardens
Smith Chas. E. 21 Bournemouth Gardens
Smith Charles H. 54 Holywell Avenue
Smith Herbert James, 5 Queen's Road
Smith John Addison, 100 Marine Avenue
Smith John Hopper, 32 Queen's Road
Smith Mrs. Westly, 50 Marine Avenue
Smith Roger Bickerton, 4 Kensington Gardens
Snow Geo. Stewart, 28 The Gardens
Snowball Malcolm, 31 Hawthorn Gardens
Soden-Bird William C. 46 Queen's Road
Somerville Thomas Victor O.B.E., M.C.
    Gately Ho. Front Street
Spark David C. 14 Holywell Avenue
Spears Fredk. Thos. 79 Holywell Avenue
Spedding William Dransfield, 1 Elmwood
    Road
Spowart William, 19 Cromer Gardens
Stansfield George H. Studley Mount,
    Marine Avenue
Stewart Jas. 1 Tynedale Avenue
Stienlet Pascal J. 109 Marine Avenue
Stoker Arthur P. 52 Holywell Avenue
Storey Ralph, 10 The Avenue
Summersby Robert A. 40 Holywell Avenue
Sutor Chas.W. Claremont, Osborne Gardens
Tassie Archibald, 57 Holywell Avenue

Tate John, 22 Holywell Avenue
Tatham Duncan, 9 St. George's Crescent
Taylor Edwd. The Villa, Balmoral Gardens
Taylor Ernest Meins, 21 Queen's Road
Taylor George, Cranleigh, Osborne Gardens
Taylor George Ellis, 15 The Gardens
Taylor Miss, 30 King's Road
Teasdale George, 1 Osborne Gardens
Teasdale Ralph, 28 Beverley Park
Ternell Charles Robt. 8 The Avenue
Thompson Arth. 2 Bournemouth Gardens
Thompson George C. 44 Queen's Road
Thornton Geo. Thos. 42 Queen's Road
Tinwell Mrs. 16 Beverley Road
Todd Capt. Ernest Henry, 2 Cauldwell Close
Todd Charles Edward, 5 Beverley Road
Todd Harrison, 15 Cromer Gardens
Todd John W. Beverley Park
Towns Thomas, 36 St. George's Crescent
Traylen Anthony Kilby, 10 Beverley Road
Turnbull Edwin, Priorhaugh, Hawthorn
    Gardens
Turnbull Frederick, 94 Marine Avenue
Turnbull James, 12 The Avenue
Turton James, Bygate Road
Twaddell James L. 19 Holywell Avenue
Tweedy Ivan, 4 Evesham Gardens
Verity Charles Frederick, The Villas,
    Balmoral Gardens
Walker David, 8 St. George's Crescent
Walker Jas Alfd. 10 Kensington Gardens
Walker John Robert, 15 Bournemouth
    Gardens
Walker Mrs. 10 Bournemouth Gardens
Wallis Robt. 36 Holywell Avenue
Wanless Geo. Thos. 69 Queen's Road

Ward Fras. Aislabie, 21 Holywell Avenue
Ward Henry, 23 Queen's Road
Watson Capt. Edward Hubert, 4 Hawthorn
    Gardens
Watson Jn. Wm. 6 Bournemouth Gardens
Watson Joseph, St. George's, Marine Avenue
Watson Mrs. L. J. B. 33 Queen's Road
Watt Mrs. 84 Marine Avenue
Wear William Thomas, 11 Holywell Avenue
Webster Fred B. 10 Beverley Park
Weddle William, 14 The Avenue
Weightman Thos. S. 19 Hawthorn Gardens
West William Thomas, Woodcroft,
    Eastfield Avenue
White John Francis, 49 Queen's Road
White Mrs. 55 Marine Avenue
Whitfield James, Breffni, The Grove
Whitton Charles, 35 Hawthorn Gardens
Widdows Hubert B. 3 Kensington Gardens
Wilkinson Edward, 85 Marine Avenue
Wilkinson Fletcher, 42 Holywell Avenue
Wilkinson Jn. L. Shield La. Blyth Road
Wilkinson Percy Norman, 10 Holywell
    Avenue
Williams C. D., B.A. 111 Marine Avenue
Wilson Haigh O.B.E. 23 Bournemouth
    Gardens
Wilson Herbert, 27 Bournemouth Gardens
Wood Evelyn, 20 Beverley Road
Wood John William, 72 Marine Avenue
Wood Mrs. Carnbrae, Front Street
Wright John, 12 Holywell Avenue
Wright Mark R., M.A., J.P. 17 St. George's
    Crescent
Young Thomas, 90 Marine Avenue
Young William, 1 King's Road

Nos. 3 to 12 Osborne Gardens as seen from the site of Souter Park, c.1922.

COMMERCIAL

Allard's Stores Ltd. (Grocers), 50 Eastbourne Gardens

Anderson Margaret Mrs., (Outfitter), St. Ronan's Road

Atkinson Eleanor Miss, (Masseuse) 14 Brighton Grove

Belettie, (Draper) St. Ronan's Road

Bennett Jn. (Grocer) 14 St. Ronan's Road

Bishop Frederick, (Tailor) 16a St. Ronan's Road

Blacklock Alfred, (Shopkeeper) 18 St. Ronan's Road

Bolton George, (Fruiterer) 49 Ilfracombe Gardens

Bonner Henry Victor, (Butcher) 6 St. Ronan's Road

Brewis Snowdon, (Farmer) Newsteads

Brown Henry, (Painter) 5 Melrose Avenue

Bullock W. J. & Sons, (Bakers) St. Ronan's Road

Carless Jack, (Boot Repairer) Marmion Terrace

Carrick's (Dairy) Ltd. 7 St.Ronan's Road

Charlton Albert, (Dairyman) St. Ronan's Road

Charlton Edward D. (Market Gardener) Dickies Holm

Clark John, (Watchmaker) 48 Ilfracombe Gardens

Close Tom, (Farmer) Seatonville Farm

Cragg Thos. (Confectioner) 17 Front Street

Cunningham William M.B., Ch.B., D.P.H. (Physician & Surgeon) firm: (Leiper & Cunningham) Coquet House, Marine Avenue

Curry Annie Miss, (Draper) St. Ronan's Road

Davidson Joseph, (Blacksmith)

Davison John, (Monkseaton Arms P.H.)

Dawson John M. (Builder) 1 Claremont Gardens

Dawson William, (Hairdresser) 16 St. Ronan's Road

Dowser Thomas M.C., F.R.C.S.Irel. (Physician & Surgeon) 54 Marine Ave

Duncan W. Ltd. (Grocers) 10 St. Ronan's Road & 45 Ilfracombe Gardens

Dunn Charles, (Farmer) Red House Farm

English Elizabeth Mrs., (Shopkeeper) 48 Eastbourne Gardens

Finlay & Co. Limited, (Tobacconists) Railway Station

Finlay Henry J. (Grocer) Ilfracombe Gardens

Forster Jas. (Costumier) 14 Queen's Road

Fryer John M. (Auctioneer) Stoneyhurst, Deneholm

Gofton Bros, (Builders & Contractors) Hill Crest

Gofton Thomas T. (Farmer) Burnt House

Gray Edward, (Coal Merchant) Ships Cot

Haimes George William, (Shopkeeper) r. Coldwell Lane

Hastings Arthur Linay, (Builder) Abbotsford Park

Hedley Fdk. (Confectioner) 21 St. Ronan's Road

Heslop E. Brinton L.D.S. Edin. (Dentist) Aldersyde, Marine Avenue

Holdsworth Walter, (Boot Repairer) 14a, St. Ronan's Road

Holmes Fred, (Builder) 89 Marine Avenue

Horton Wm. (Grocer) 2 St. Ronan's Road

Eastbourne Gardens, looking east, c.1920. The general dealers shop to the left is number 48 Eastbourne Gardens which was run by a Mrs Elizabeth English. It has since been converted to a house. The shop to the extreme right is Bygate Dairy Stores (No 45 Eastbourne Gardens) which was run by Mr Joseph Scott, beyond which is Samuel Sims fruiterers shop at No. 43. Construction work is still evident in the distance to the south side of the street.

Ilfracombe Dairy Co. 55 Ilfracombe Gardens

Imisson Horace Benjamin, (Butcher) Marmion Terrace

James Henry, (Farmer) East Farm

Jamieson's Pharmacies Limited. St. Ronan's Road

Jarman Cyril, (Cabinet Maker) 12 Front Street

Johnson Dorothy Miss (Confectioner) 4 St. Ronan's Road

Johnson John, (Jobbing Gardener) 50 Ilfracombe Gardens

Kelley Lydie Mrs. (Draper) 8 St. Ronan's Road

Laidler Jn. Thos. (Fishmonger) 20 St Ronan's Road

Laidler Jn. Thos. (Fruiterer) 22, St. Ronan's Road

Leaders (Newcastle-on-Tyne) Ltd. (Grocers) Marmion Terrace

Leech Thomas Davison, (China & Glass Dealer) 1 St. Ronan's Road

Leiper & Cunningham, (Physicians & Surgeons) 76 Marine Avenue

Leiper James Alexander M.B., Ch.B. Glas. (Physician & Surgeon) firm; Leiper & Cunningham, 76 Marine Avenue

Lishman Thomas, (Fruiterer) 11 St. Ronan's Road

Lonie James, (Taxation Consultant) 3 Claremont Gardens

Lowrey Jane Mrs. (Draper) 3 & 5 Abbotsford Park

Mackinlay Norman Blackwood L.D.S. Edin. (Dental Surgeon), 56 Marine Avenue

McPherson John E. & Son, Black Horse P.H. Front Street

Marshall & Brown, (Bakers) Post Office, 47 Eastbourne Gardens

Middlemiss Thomas Wm. (Sanitary Engineer) Glenville, Dene Bank

Miller Jas. (Fruiterer) 12 St. Ronan's Road

Mount Preparatory School (Miss C. Glashan – Principal) 23 Front Street

Mountain Bertram H., F.B.O.A. (Ophthalmic Optician) 17 Cromer Gardens

Nicholson & Mitchell, (Physicians & Surgeons) Shellacres, Marine Avenue

Nicholson John Gibb M.A., M.B., Ch.B. (Physician & Surgeon) firm; Nicholson & Mitchell, & Medical Officer & Public Vaccinator, Whitley District, Tynemouth Union, Shellacres, Marine Avenue

Old Sewer Gas Lamps are still evident in the village, and although prominent and visible, they are largely passed by unnoticed, however they are covered in a separate section on page 86.

An interesting metal post, dating to the late 1800s is evident at the entrance to the narrow alleyway which connects Marine Avenue to Hawthorn Gardens.

Two heavy weathered oak gatepost pillars stand at the entrance to the pedestrian bridge crossing the railway lines at the end of Windsor Road next to East Avenue. Two further pillars were once situated opposite, on the Uplands side of the bridge however they were removed during the 1960s. It is apparent that these posts once housed wooden gates, perhaps to prevent cattle or farm animals straying across the bridge to the neighbouring field.

Two stone pillars situated next to 59 Seatonville Road also mark the entrance to an old pathway which once led to the former Burnt House Nurseries and Frankland Mount which is also covered under Burnt House Farm in Monkseaton Volume One.

Even streets and buildings are sometimes not readily noticed. For example, a fairly insignificant street; Victoria Place runs off Bygate Road and leads to two otherwise hidden houses behind Monkseaton Front Street; namely Seaton House and Victoria Cottage.

Further west on Earsdon Road, Newsteads Farmhouse also remains inconspicuous standing close to West Monkseaton Station, and not far away is Earsdon Square, the block of former Police Houses standing next to the present Hunting Lodge Pub.

Frankland Mount for example which stands in its own grounds is almost hidden from view, enclosed by Frankland Drive, Newlands Avenue and Mount Close.

Slightly further afield, an unusual flat pillar box dating to the reign of Queen Victoria is set into the wall of the former council depot on Shields Road at Hillheads.

Even a cracked pavement at the corner of Seatonville Road and Canberra Avenue provides a clue to the existence of the old Whitley and Monkseaton Urban District

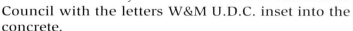
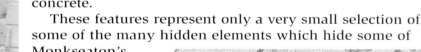

Council with the letters W&M U.D.C. inset into the concrete.

These features represent only a very small selection of some of the many hidden elements which hide some of Monkseaton's interesting history. There are of course many more which continue to remain hidden or unassuming. How many more can you find?

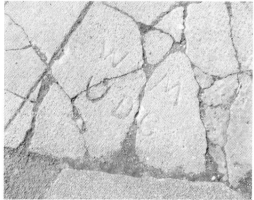

ROYAL VISIT TO MONKSEATON, 1954

On 29th October 1954, the Royal Train pulled into Monkseaton Station. On board, the recently crowned young Queen Elizabeth, accompanied by Prince Philip came to visit Whitley Bay and Tynemouth as part of the post-coronation celebrations.

This visit came just six months after the Royal Charter of Incorporation had been granted on 14th April 1954 when Whitley Bay became known as the Borough of Whitley Bay.

A huge amount of preparation for the Royal visit included over 30 council workers and gardeners starting very early in the morning to complete all the decorations which included hanging baskets and displays throughout the town.

The porter's room at Monkseaton Station was used as a storage area for the plants, and six-year-old Linda Dale of Whitley Bay was chosen to present the Queen with a bouquet.

One of the features which was specially constructed for the visit was a decorative archway which was erected across Marine Avenue next to Souter Park, accompanied by rows of coloured buntings.

Right: Marine Avenue is dressed for the occasion of the Royal visit in 1954.

The Royal Train waits in the sidings of Monkseaton Station in 1954. Behind, buntings decorate Norham Road as crowds peer over the fence in the background.

MONKSEATON MEMORIES

The following three accounts are personal recollections from contributors who have submitted their memories to North Shields Library Club's Remembering the Past, Resourcing the Future project – www.memoriesnorthtyne.org.uk

The articles are based on the memories of the individuals, some of which contain factual inaccuracies. For publishing reasons, it has also been necessary to edit some of the articles slightly. Any opinions expressed however are purely those of the contributors.

GROWING UP IN MONKSEATON

Crawford Park Tennis Court nets rusted away in the Second World War and the courts were derelict. My brother and his pals used them as a dirt track like a motorbike track but raced their pedal cycles around in big circles. One day he went down on one knee like a real dirt track rider and put a hole in the flesh of his knee. My mother was fairly tough but she nearly fainted when she saw a trace of bone at the bottom of his knee hole. He got patched up and soon was his usual smiling self though. Courting couples got behind the Crawford Park tennis pavilion, some Melbourne Crescent residents got some rare sights through their back garden fences. Melbourne Crescent gradient was quite good for sledging but Seatonville Crescent was better. Rockcliffe Rugby Ground's hill was best of all but it was a long walk for our little legs. Eight of us went to Rockcliffe one cold frosty and snowy night with three sledges, it was great but I fell off a sledge and got sundry painful bruises and they were even more painful next day. We must have looked like Scott's Antarctic Expedition, we felt like it too, but the frosty snow made the sledges easy to pull. The snow was so cold and powdery it would not make snowballs.

Bromley Avenue was a swamp before the houses were built. About 1935 the builders put a corduroy road of railway sleepers down so their horses and carts would not sink in. All new house building stopped in the Second World War with two houses half built. Along with some friends, and some of the Melbourne and Seatonville kids we took up the sleepers and built log cabin forts with them then pelted each other at a range of thirty feet

Bromley Field was once a part of Seatonville Farm, and was known as 'The Fleets'.

with clods of earth. Germonimo! In the war the Bromley playing field (which then extended over Appletree Gardens) was two large fields with yellow gorse bushes dotted over the western half with a hedge and ditch, which widened into two ponds extending east from Bromley Avenue. Two drains came down from Seatonville Road and the ditch from what is now Burnt House Road. These drains were lined bottom, top and either side with thick sandstone flags to give a water course 2 ft x 1 ft high. Some top stones had fallen in to form little ponds. All the water drained to an old closed mineshaft under what is now the east side of Appletree Gardens. This was paradise for toads, frogs water boatmen and sundry other crawlies and swimmie's as there was always around six inches of standing water in these open and closed drains. You could hear water falling some fifteen foot down the collapsed mine shaft and I often wondered what lived down there. A Mr. Tait and others had overgrown allotments along the edge of Seatonville Road. I thought they were derelict and harvested his potatoes for my mother. Mr Tait who was also our next door neighbour said we could keep some but he would appreciate it if I would pass his spuds over the fence for his Sunday dinner, which I did. His son Jack was the manager of Whitley Athletic Football Team after coming out of the RAF.

About 1947 the building of Appletree Gardens started and Springfield Grove recommenced. The frogs' crawlies' and most swimmie's had emigrated, but I was concerned for the remaining toads so I caught all I could find and put them in our back garden. My mother thought I had maybe three, but it was more like fifteen. I sank a large old aluminium fish pan full of water in a corner for them, all the neighbours one after another said 'we have got toads in our garden', others said 'funny so have we'. History repeats itself, last month I had 17 frogs in the garden. If Appletree Gardens ever disappears down a big hole now you know why. Only I hope there is no mine shaft under our house! I know a chap that this happened to; luckily his wife and himself were at work when their house caved in.

Where the terraced houses on Cauldwell Lane stand (behind the upper part of Paignton Avenue), in 1938 this was just a hilly rough field, then the council built an underground air raid shelter about 30ft x 70ft with a concrete tank of water (for fire fighting) on the roof. By 1944 air raids were long since over and the shelter was derelict. We dismantled some of the bunks and used up some fence nails to build an 8ft x 3ft boat to sail on the tanks mini lake. We had trouble making it watertight, we covered it with Hessian from the bunks but needed some tar (polythene would have done but it hadn't been invented). Unfortunately we couldn't track down any road repairs taking place! The boat floated but as soon as one person climbed in it sank. The water was 4ft deep and cold. We considered making a boy-carrying glider but sawing the wood was too much work.

We did not mean to be vandals we just were practical, adventurous, kids wanting to make things and make life more interesting. Like the couple of days we carted a lot of bricks 100 yards from a building site to BriarDene stream and dammed it up. We wanted a midsummer swim in fresh water not salt water. It would not be more than 3ft deep, but the dam leaked like a sieve and we flooded 30 square yards of the golf course – but not a green fortunately.

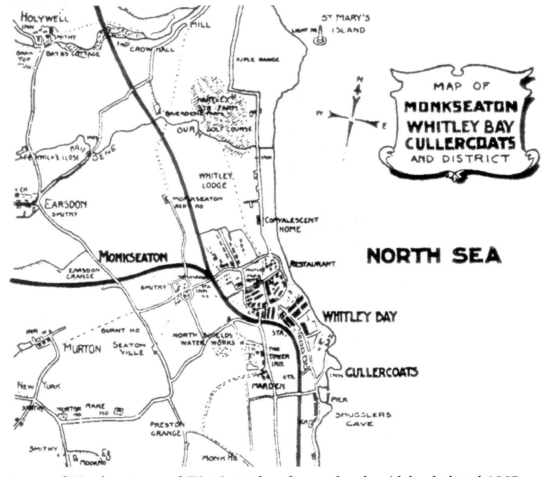

A map of Monkseaton and District, taken from a local guidebook dated 1907.

A 1950s advertisement for R.A. Gofton, Front Street, Monkseaton.

A late 1930s advertisement for J.L. Johnston (Monkseaton Village Garage).

PEOPLE IN MONKSEATON

Mr. Rab Jewel (he and all his family have now died out) lived down our street and worked during the war at Swan Hunter's. His father, his brother and himself built four houses, numbered 51 to 57 Wembley Avenue, for members of his family about 1926. When you examine these houses closely you can see that the design and workmanship is of an unusually high standard; 'Old man Jewel' was a master craftsman. Hector and Rab, the brothers, built some houses in Selwyn Avenue but had to leave them unfinished in the war as they couldn't get licenses to buy doors, floorboards and fittings. I got a real telling off from Rab for playing in his houses, as without floorboards they were dangerous. The Brights lived at number 57, Hector and his wife and her college friend Miss Younger lived at 55, old Miss Jewel their sister at 53 and Rab and his wife at 51. Hector's wife, Miss Younger and old Miss Jewel were teachers. Miss Jewel never went to college and when she left school aged 14 (about 1890) she went to help in an infants school, served an apprenticeship as a teacher and was certificated as such. She taught at New York (near Shiremoor) Infants School.

In the winters of 1941 and 1947 we had a lot of snow that stayed for nearly a month, Miss Jewel got to her school by walking along the tops of the Rake Lane hedges that were just showing through the deep snow. She always walked to and fro from school even when past retirement age, about three miles a day, rain and shine. No wonder she lived to be about 90 years of age. During the war many teachers were called up for the Forces so many others came out of retirement. We had an English master who was about 75 years old and rather frail but his handwriting was copper plate, artistic and near perfect.

Rab Jewel was a builder handyman but in the war was sent to work at Swan Hunter's Shipyard. He was always making things in his garage, where he had an old lathe and a drilling machine. These were ancient – maybe dating back to 1902 – their motors were partly open and threw out sparks when running, which fascinated my

93

brother and I. He made my mother a poker like a sword out of steel copper and bronze, a very artistic and serviceable piece of work. I thought it useful for chasing Germans also! One fine sunny evening Rab was just walking out of West Monkseaton Railway Station when he tripped and there was an almighty clang! He had a sheet of copper wound around his body under his mackintosh with string like braces over his shoulders to support the copper jacket. The string snapped! A rather sheepish Rab struggled along Eardson Road, then down our street clutching the copper jacket partly visible under his now open raincoat. Now we knew where he got his raw materials! He built a model Mississippi paddle steamer with a real boiler and steam engine in his garage workshop. It was about three feet long and he occasionally steamed it on Tynemouth Lake.

ROUND AND ABOUT IN MONKSEATON

Bygate School had a crab apple tree, the apples were small and looked very nice, but taste them once and you would never do so again as they were amazingly bitter and sour. They would make an interesting cider though. The second St Peter's Church was next door to Bygate School but got demolished by a bomb. The first temporary St Peter's Church was in what is now the Methodist Chapel before the old church was built about 1880. My Mother took me to Bygate School twice a day and twice a day collected me. Before each return journey she lifted my brother out of his pram and put two bits of broken church stone under him. Over the months she built quite a nice rockery in our garden, the only consecrated one in the area!

South West Farm Stack Yard, Chapel Lane.

The buildings opposite Bygate School (now the Spar Shop etc), formed a working farm in the 1940s. The little stone shed opposite Jenkinson's Glass shop housed a bull. Us kids shouted rude words at the bull whereupon it would charge the wall with an almighty crash – very impressive and a bit scary. Spar's car park had a high chicken wire around most of it and housed Bantams (about half the size of hens) but much showier, really beautiful birds. They looked more intelligent – especially the Cocks.

Tyne Taxis had a large fleet of coffee coloured Austin cars, operated from the back of Kelly's DIY. As the cars got too old after seven years or so they were not all replaced so this business contracted. One day upon leaving school at lunchtime there was sound of a crash by the Black Horse Hotel, I went to have a look. Amazingly the front end of a No. 17 double decker bus was down a big hole in the road, the bus was tilted at nearly 45 degrees. The sewer by the bus stop had caved in. The last straw was the force of the bus braking for its stop probably. One night I went down for fish and chips to the then chippy, next to The Fold, on my bike. Whilst I was in the Chippy someone cut the wire of my bike dynamo lights into short strips. Much annoyed I got on my bike and after riding ten yards or so a policeman stopped me and told me off for riding without lights. He was surprised in turn to be well and truly told off (by a nine year old boy) for not keeping his eyes open and catching vandals. I was very angry indeed. The Fold was a large unkempt garden with a big house at the back and a cottage on either side of the garden, originally it was a farm. About four hundred years ago Monkseaton Village sprang from about five farms in a defensive ring, like a wagon train being attacked by

Redskins. These farms being longitudinal were said to be Saxon, i.e. from before 1066. Perhaps they were built this way to repel Viking attacks? On the corner of St Ronan's Road and St George's Crescent was another recently derelict farm in the 1940s where I used to lark about with friends. The Spar shop was farm number three, number four was at the back of the Brewery behind the Monkseaton Arms. A hundred yards west of Whitley High School was another farm with attendant cottages. In the late 1940s Whitley UDC bought BriarDene a very pleasant little picnic spot, and vandalised it into a council tip. Council dust cart lorries used to race down the cart track from the end of Deneholm to their BriarDene tip, totally wrecking the farmers approach track and putting walker, horse riders and cyclists in fear of their lives and covering the farm in fine ash. No wonder the farmer sold out for building Beaumont Park Estate.

The Fold, Monkseaton, c 1910.

Two children dressed in their Sunday best, pose for the photographer near Chapel Lane.

Also available from Summerhill Books

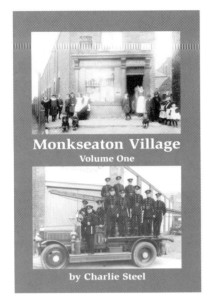

Monkseaton Village
Volume One

by Charlie Steel

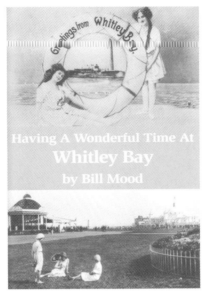

Having A Wonderful Time At **Whitley Bay**
by Bill Mood

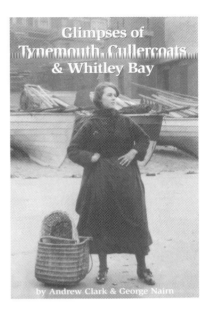

Glimpses of **Tynemouth, Cullercoats** & Whitley Bay

by Andrew Clark & George Nairn

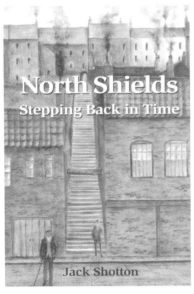

North Shields
Stepping Back in Time

Jack Shotton

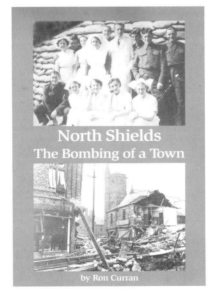

North Shields
The Bombing of a Town

by Ron Curran

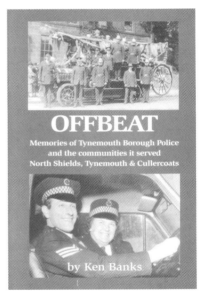

OFFBEAT

Memories of Tynemouth Borough Police
and the communities it served
North Shields, Tynemouth & Cullercoats

by Ken Banks

Wallsend Best

A Personal Experience of the Rising Sun Colliery
by Ron Curran

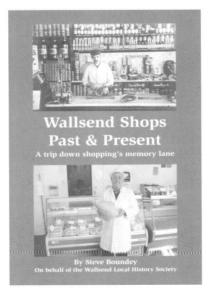

Wallsend Shops Past & Present
A trip down shopping's memory lane

By Steve Boundey
On behalf of the Wallsend Local History Society

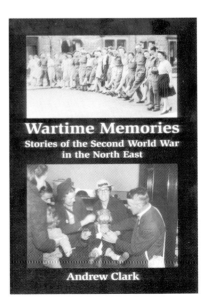

Wartime Memories
Stories of the Second World War
in the North East

Andrew Clark

www.summerhillbooks.co.uk